Odd-Coupling

The creative and innovative power
from recombining resources

Odd-Coupling

The creative and innovative power
from recombining resources

Christopher Loughlan

First published in 2013 by
Pi Publishing House
www.odd-coupling.co.uk

ISBN 978-0-9575016-0-7

Cover design by John Chipperfield

Contents

Preface
From Chris Dobrowolski

When I was invited to write this preface for a book on idea creation and business development, I thought it was strange because I don't have any background in business whatsoever. It was only after I found out the title and the concept of the book that I began to understand the relevance of my contribution. Instead of business I went to college and studied art which, in the context of this particular book, isn't as irrelevant a background or "odd coupling" as it would first appear.

Art education in the early nineties was as philosophical as it was visual and as such encouraged us to question everything we did. My personal response to this approach led me to question the very institution I was studying in. In my first year of study I collected driftwood from the riverbank and built a boat so that I could get in it and use it to escape from Art College. The boat worked but I was an inexperienced sailor. To cut a very long story short – my escape attempt failed. However, this experience led to a whole series of other projects on a similar vehicle theme that became a long tale of trial, error disaster and 'success' that culminated with an aeroplane made from tea chests and newspaper that actually worked.

The plane I designed, built and flew

The vehicles have been shown in a number of art galleries; putting the vehicle back into the art environment it was made to escape from, was not only contradictory but also laid the work open to appropriation by the very system it was built to protest against. I have subsequently been invited to talk about what I have made to people outside of the art world that is to the general public, students and business. In this context the work has become an example of creativity and thinking differently. Contributing to creativity in this context has been more rewarding and sustainable than a show at art galleries. This activity, moreover, performs some sort of educational and cultural function within society.

This book on odd-coupling of resources will challenge your thinking on idea creation and the linkage of ideas to entrepreneurship and business development.

Acknowledgments

I would like to express thanks to many people who have helped bring this book to fruition. In particular my thanks go to Li Quan Founding Director, Save China's Tigers; Professor Mutya Subrahmanyam, India; Dr Sangli Maharashtra, India; Dr, Makoto Imai Shiga University, Japan; Michael Lewis, USA; Bart Weetjeyns and William Deed of Apopo, Belgium; Dr Andreas Schieber, University of Bonn, Germany; Richard Yemm and Deborah Smith, Pelamis Wave Power, Edinburgh, Scotland, UK; David Harris, Duncan Bishop, Cambridge Consultants, Cambridge UK; Sun Pharma, Mumbai, India; David Harris, Team Consulting , Cambridge UK; Paula Hagadon, Hesco, UK; the family of Jimi Heselden, UK; Richard Jacobs, USA; Jayne Williams, Will Crawford and Peter Brewin of Concrete Canvas, UK; Doug Stewart, Aberdeen, Scotland; Paul D'Orleans, USA; the National Museum of Northern Ireland; Jane ni Dhulchaointigh, UK; Dr Julian Brown, UK; Dean at Pest Control (UK); Marian Edmunds, NSW Australia.

I would like to acknowledge a number of people who contributed to the production of this book. Grit Hartung (UK) who introduced me to the relationship between design and meaning. To a number of friends who critiqued working drafts: Cia Durante (UK), Jonathan Evans (UK) and Colin Jones (Australia). Finally, to Guardian Media Group Masterclass colleagues who critiqued and helped bring along the book: Christopher Shevlin, Kath Houston , Mike Daligan, Murray Armstrong, Lynne Suo, Brigid Shaunessy, Martine McDonagh, and Rod Bilton.

Illustrations and photographs

Chapter 1, photos courtesy of Apopo, Belgium; chapter 2 photo of baseball courtesy of Rawlings Inc USA; images of tigers in chapter 3 courtesy of Li Quan and Save China 's Tigers; photo of smoke detector in chapter 5 courtesy of Seems Inc, Tokyo; photograph of Abbot Inhaler in chapter courtesy of Primary Care Respiratory Journal; photograph of a repaired boot in chapter 7 courtesy of Sugru; photographs of the motorcycle frame and 'The Benial' in chapter 8 courtesy of National Museums, Northern Ireland; photograph in chapter 9 courtesy of Hesco Bastion; photograph in chapter 10 courtesy of Concrete Canvas; photographs in chapter 11 courtesy of Doug Stewart; photograph in chapter 12 courtesy of Dr Julian Brown; images in chapter 13 courtesy of Pest Control (UK); images and plates in chapter 15 courtesy of Babcox & Wilcox/Cambridge University Press; and finally photographs in the preface and adieu sections of the book, courtesy of Chris Dobrowolski.

Introduction

Odd-coup•ling *noun*
1: the joining of things, something unusual, out of the ordinary, unexpected
2: the (re) combination of un-related resources to produce a new product or service that adds value to society.

I wanted to write a different sort of book on entrepreneurship and enterprise. My approach was to start with two fundamental concepts: what are human beings good at and the basic human need to be recognised for the value we contribute through work to society. Research from the field of health promotion has confirmed that we like to do valuable work and be recognised by others (those who supposedly "manage" us) for this contribution – money incidentally rarely comes out on top in relation to key factors that concern why we work.

When Studs Terkel wrote about the meaning of work, he researched his theme by interviewing hundreds of people across America. He described his work as: 'a search, too, for daily meaning as well as daily bread, for recognition as well as cash, for astonishment rather than torpor; in short, for a sort of life rather than a Monday through Friday sort of dying'[1].

This book has been written to search and explore the relationship between ideas and entrepreneurship. In part, in writing about these ideas, I have been astonished by human ingenuity and innovation – the bedrock of entrepreneurship. In particular, the book focuses on odd-coupling, the innovative use or the combination of (often) unusual resources.

I define odd-coupling as the combination of one or more characteristics of a resource to help or solve a problem or issue in a different area of interest or physical locale. Paley writing in The Art of Invention talks about the concept of envisioning, where you are looking at 'areas or technologies that are unfamiliar to you....to gain contiguous expertise'. He goes on to say that 'often invention comes from a connection made from two completely unrelated areas'[2].

Biomimicry is but another example of odd-coupling. This is a new science that studies nature's models and then imitates or takes inspiration from these designs and processes to solve human problems[3]. Nature has perfected systems and processes for 3.8 billion years and it's always with a lot less energy, a lot less material, and negligible toxins – basically a lot better. Human beings however have demonstrated a terrible track record of maintaining environmental balance in trying to solve problems .

A classic example of biomimicry is the development of velcro fastener from the original observation by a Swiss engineer, George de Mestral, that wild burrs (plant seed sacs) stuck very well to his dog's coat and to his trousers. A more up to date example relates to the influence of the kingfisher's beak in the design of the shinkansen (the Japanese 'white bullet' train); the train uses fifteen per cent less electricity and minimises the frontal pressure wave resulting in greater stability and less noise pollution.

Once you start to generate ideas through odd-coupling the practice becomes easier; besides, it is free and unlimited. As Malcolm Gladwell described in his book[4] exploring factors of success, what you make of your ideas is largely down to hours of practice and crucially the support, advice and opportunity out there. The skill of odd-coupling comes from generation of ideas and taking your ideas to market by identifying which resources you need and how to get them.

This book is a collection of short stories, or 'cameo' pieces, to add insight into the practice and outcomes of odd-coupling. From credentialed rats to trading on the stats, from alarming mustard to healing potato skins, the examples all portray an ability to look at things or problems in a new light and produce ideas which can be tested. The subsequent products or outcomes don't simply fall out of the sky but are a direct result of one's craft or art, perseverance, tenacity to draw positives from so-called 'failures', the re-combining of unusual resources and, of course, to be in the right place at the right time to benefit from luck or happenchance.

Each chapter starts with a visual or one sort or another embodying the resource(s) that were re-combined in a different setting or locale. This format was not merely for design purposes but to emphasise the point that entrepreneurs generally develop a strong visual sense in helping them either see a solution to a problem or be able to pose the question in a different way and hence come up with a unique solution.

Before you read each chapter, you could set yourself the task of thinking of the characteristics of the resource(s) and predict or anticipate what each odd-coupling was to present to us.

1

Credentialed rats:
mission ready

This story is a classic example of odd-coupling. Ask anyone a decade ago that rats would be credentialed and the response would have been that such talk is fanciful; ask anyone that a credentialed rat would be part of a highly cost-effective mine clearing team and the response would be incredulous. Until that is Bart Weetjens set up a rat detection agency called Apopo that has pioneered a unique approach which is proving to be a highly sustainable solution to a debilitating and deadly war legacy in African countries.

Landmines are explosive material contained in casings of metal, plastic or wood that detonate from the pressure of a footstep (anti-personnel mine) or a passing vehicle (anti-tank mine). They are relatively cheap to produce and require minimal skill to deploy. It is estimated that there are between 70 and 80 million landmines in the ground in one-third of the world's nations.[1] More than 100 million antipersonnel landmines are active in some of the poorest countries of the world.

More worryingly from a longer term perspective, a further 100 million landmines are held in stockpiles.[2] In Mozambique alone, it is estimated that there are three million mines.[3] Landmines are indiscriminate weapons that maim or kill 15,000 to 20,000 civilians every year. Landmines pose a threat on two levels. There is the cost to human lives in particular to young children; there is also the wider cost in terms of economic growth and longer term investment. The deleterious economic effects of landmines are the loss of accessible and arable land, strains on the health system, loss of productive labour, inhibition of the repatriation of refugees, and obstruction of economic development. Moreover countries like Mozambique and Somalia have had to continually rely on external aid and expertise; such expertise being associated with a high tech solutions to the problem.

Just how good is a rat's nose for detecting smells? Pretty good actually. Olfaction or sense of smell was developed by animals through evolution to aid communication with the environment such that they can both detect danger and identify prey. Dogs and rats have a highly developed capability to detect and identify odorant molecules even at minute concentration. It has been shown that olfactory receptors (ORs) that specifically bind odorant molecules are encoded by the largest gene family sequenced in mammals so far. Quignon and colleagues demonstrated that a dog has 1058 OR related genes whilst our erstwhile rat has 1493.[4]

The training of the rat begins with a process of socialisation. At four weeks old, young rats are weaned from their mothers and APOPO's trainers begin to familiarise them to the smells, sounds, and environments of the human world. These processes help the rats learn to adapt and reduce any fear of experiences they might encounter in the field, in training or during operations. At six weeks, 'click training' (so-called Pavlovian response) begins where the rat learns to associate a click sound with a food reward – usually banana or peanuts. After two weeks training, the rats learns that click results in gaining food, and are now ready to be trained on a target scent. In laboratory conditions when they meet the target scent (explosive) a click is made and food is presented hence training the rat to associate explosive material detection with food. These rats then progress to controlled conditions in the field (open land) where the rat is introduced to its trainer and to the wearing of a leash; their job is now to detect target mines that have been planted in what will be live or natural conditions. Having undergone this transition phase, the rats then progress to their 'examination'. Guided by their trainer, the rats have to clear four hundred square metres and detect all the planted mines. Only when they have done so will the rat become credentialed and engage in mine detection for real. It should be added that being light-weight, there is no risk of the rats detonating a live mine. The training and examination takes nine months and costs approximately six thousand euros to complete.

The detection programme is highly cost effective: it can clear land at a cost of 1.18$ per square metre which is a sixty per cent improvement on standard operating costs. Eleven African governments have endorsed the rat detection scheme. The programme involves upskilling local people to contribute to not only minimising the risk of disability and death but to the longer term economic growth of the region.

The application of this detection process has now moved to early detection of tuberculosis through the rats trained ability to 'recognise' infected sputum of patients. It is highly cost effective route to treatment and prevention of further infection.

From an early age Bart exhibited two passions: a love of rodents and a love of Africa, its culture and its people. He also exhibited a true entrepreneurial flair in youth by breeding rodents and selling them on to local pet shops. His later career in production engineering could not fulfil an inner desire to contribute something more positive in society: to tackling something which was causing real-time death and severe disability.

He is keen to stress that his activities are about people, vulnerable people and coming up with sustainable solutions to what must seem intractable problems. His view on using and applying resources resonates strongly with one of the founding principles of biomimicry namely nature as mentor: 'a way of viewing and valuing nature. It introduces an era based not on what we can extract from the natural world, but on what we can learn from it'.[5] Therefore I will leave you here with the words of the founder of Apopo: 'keep on challenging (your) perceptions of resources around you (be they environmental, technical, animal, human) respectfully harmonising with them in order to foster a sustainable world'.[6]

2

Trading on the stats:
an unwelcome paradigm for sports coaches

Up until the 1980s, general managers of major league baseball teams relied heavily on an extended 'family' of former baseball players known as talent scouts. The practice and related rituals had been unquestioned and unquestionable – that is until a certain Billy Beane, general manager of the Oakland A's, came on the scene. But before I expound on the unusual coupling, a short discourse on the characteristics of American baseball (I suppose some sort of an immediate apology is needed here to baseball aficionados in what is an all too feeble attempt to summarise baseball as: a player (hitter) with a bat, a thrower (pitcher) and out-fielders those players who go collect the ball).[1] I hasten to add that this story of odd-coupling is more to do with the actual scoring system and subsequent analyses, and the response from baseball managers than the intricacies of play itself.

There was a clear case of imbalance in major league baseball. As Michael Lewis pointed out in his successful book 'Moneyball': 'At the opening of 2002 season, the richest team, the NY Yankees, had a payroll of some 126 million dollars while the two poorest teams, the Oakland A's and the Tampa Bay Devil Rays, had payrolls of less than one third of that amount, about forty million dollars'.[2] The assumption and wisdom was that only the well-to -do clubs could afford the better players. Against this backdrop was an inconvenient fact – why had the Oakland A's managed to win more regular season games than all but one of the other twenty nine teams and moreover in two play-offs had taken the richest team in baseball, the NY Yankees, to a very close call? How on earth did they do it? Michael Lewis explains: 'At the bottom of the Oakland experiment was a willingness to re-think baseball: how it is managed, how it is played, who is best suited to play, and why'. Billy Beane set about looking at the inefficiencies in the game...in essence (trying to find) a new type of knowledge or resource.

Billy Beane's yardstick did not come from developing his somewhat fractious relationship with his cadre of extended talent scouts at the club. It came from a rather different and unexpected route. In drafting in new players to the club, he was keen to use a more scientific approach to measurement and judgment rather than rely solely on the responses from his extensive back room of talent scouts. To understand the radical shift (and subsequent hostile reaction), one needs to have the basics of baseball scoring.

Baseball data conflated luck and skills and ignored a lot of what happened during a game. In any one event, the stats might record a hitter (success) and a pitcher (failed); however the fielder (defending team) and the runner (attacking team) were simply add-ons. As Michael Lewis noted: 'This was a grotesque failure of justice'.

In the 1980's two financial analysts by the name of Ken Mauriello and Jack Armbruster were working in the new field of 'derivatives'- a part of the money market where stocks and bonds were 'broken up' into many smaller parts (derivatives) to facilitate trading.[3] A lot of money could be made by trading on such derivatives. A lot of money. Each little fragment or derivative was worth a certain amount. The sum total of the many small parts had to equal the overall sum of any particular stock or bond. The prize in financial terms was being able to spot the inefficiencies in the market – where the sum of the parts didn't add to the whole. Such analysts made quantitative analysts, as opposed to gut feel, the respectable way to go about making bets in the market. In economic terms, such analysts priced risk more accurately and distributed it more efficiently- they made a new connection between inefficiency and opportunity.

Mauriello and Armbruster then got to work on the inefficiencies of recording and analyses in the baseball game.

The odd-coupling was the application of a derivative market analyses to baseball in order to produce a better indicator of player value (which for many players was in the high millions) and potential performance in the field of play. By recording as much relevant and appropriate data from any one game, they sought to assign a value to as many meaningful events that they could; this involved a complex coding that tracked velocity, trajectory and an identifier to the exact landing place of the ball. This new radical system of scoring baseball involved breaking up the game into tiny related fragments (i.e. a derivative of the game). By summing up all these derivatives, the stats could amass a sum total of player performance. This new system ignored traditional baseball statistics and attempted to take a lot of guesswork out of match analyses. The odd-coupling was expressed as follows: 'An insight born in the financial markets took root in the mind of a young man who would soon have the power to put it to use inside major league baseball'. There was now an additional level of analysis beyond guesswork, gut instinct or conventional field statistics.

The general manager of Oakland A's instigated a paradigm shift at the club and into the world of baseball. Many of his contemporaries remain challenged and hostile to such an approach. The results of the Oakland A's were tantamount to proving that the club had a better 'measure' of player performance and true potential. Billy Beane's team continued to defy the critics and outperformed many if not most of the clubs that had significant funds to attract the so-called better players. The protégés of Billy Beane were in demand and would soon gain managerial positions in clubs of reputation. Other club managers would in time, and with great reluctance, come to acknowledge that the system of player evaluation at Oakland A's was to be emulated.[4]

The main character in this account was a general manager

of a (financially) 'third rate' baseball club who struggled and battled his way to the top of his game. He was a highly driven individual who at times was described as 'maniacal' –it was unwise to be in the same room if things weren't going too well and where there was a free chair to be lobbed against an empty wall. That he knew his craft was undoubted. He was willing to take high level prolonged risk on a personal, family and team level – he assured himself with the self-belief that anything he did could only be as bad (or poor) as the status quo (such as a reliance on a cadre of retired team scouts). He placed great faith in the science of analyses and he was not afraid in being the first to do so. I will give Michael Lewis the final say: 'he appointed people who thought about baseball in a different way... who were not set in the old ways of accepting the received wisdom'. In time, Billy Beane adopted the Mauriello and Armbruster system for player analyses for the first couple of years and then, like any true entrepreneur, adopted it and used it as his own.

$$AVG = \frac{H}{AB} \quad OBP = \frac{H+BB}{PA} \quad SLUG = \frac{TB}{AB}$$

3

A different reserve:
Re-wilding an endangered species

Laohu Valley Reserve

Are there tigers in Africa? This is a popular question asked of our primary school aged children and of course the answer is naturally no. By naturally no, I mean that whilst the tiger, like all cats, can and does adapt to extremes of temperature and climate (from tropical Sumatra and Java to the snowy terrain of Siberia), nature has determined that as yet there are no tigers in South Africa – until that is Li Quan took a personal hand in matters to help save the most endangered tiger in the world. But first a short discourse on animal habitat and extinction.[1]

The presence of any animal which can only be found in a zoo (or a human controlled environment) is declared functionally extinct; thus with few or any sightings of the tiger in South China, it has recently been declared as extinct.[2] Indeed the conservation of tiger population in India and Russia was viewed in some quarters as failing.[3] It is widely accepted that if an animal is to survive and ultimately thrive, then one must look at the system in which the animal lives notably its natural habitat; any study of animal conservation is wound up in a study of the animal's natural habitat. Around ten years ago Li realised that the conservation clock was ticking down fast on the total number of tigers in captivity in China. Besides, there were no plans for declaring key areas of land for wildlife preservation and was unable to tempt international conservation experts over to China. Li came up with an extremely ambitious and highly contentious idea: to re-wild the China tiger in South Africa. The reserve, she believed, offers the best practical environment for species rescue experiences.

Within zoo conditions the basic demands of shelter and food are a given; captive tigers furthermore are conditioned to enclosed spaces, concrete surfaces and food delivered to them. Li wanted to re-wild captive tigers but she needed two vital elements to succeed: a suitable and sizeable habitat in China and what is called 'big cat' expertise. She was not able to secure the former and was cold shouldered by the latter. The basis of Li's idea was very ambitious i.e. to provide the supportive environment for them to hunt for their food and find shelter but also highly contentious by coupling these captive tigers with the land resources not somewhere remote in China but of another continent – namely Africa. The very idea was viewed as being on the 'edge of the conservation world'.[4]

In doing so, she came across a range of criticism and barriers which were political, economic, scientific and ethical. Just how do you go about persuading the government of the People's Republic of China to not only lend you a couple of tigers but moreover to giving you permission to take them to South Africa for an audacious experiment? She was able to persuade the powers that be that taking no action in the face of total extinction was not a viable option and that her plan was one way of "expediting the re-wilding of Chinese tigers", to encourage expertise into China and in identifying and preparing wildlife sites for their eventual return. A grand plan no less.

Such a bold idea would also require relatively large and sustained financial resources over a number of years. In this regard Li was able to call upon significant personal reserves as she and her husband had pursued well rewarded careers in the past.

She met with a large body of criticism from leading exponents in the field of animal welfare and conservation. This criticism covered a broad range of concerns. One of the more simplistic views put forward by the World Wild Fund for Nature was that it was an unwise investment and thought that they were in a better position to utilise Li's financial resources.[5] A more detailed critique and exposition of the main scientific and biological concerns were articulated by Gus Mills of behalf of the Carnivore Conservation Group.[6] Lastly, there was an ethical dimension in the concern that the introduction of prey as food for the newly introduced tiger to the habitat constituted an act of cruelty. At one stage, the team had a visit by the local police force to question them on their activities as they had seemingly violated a law on the introduction of live prey for the tigers; there is a bye-law which states that no animal should be forced into a condition which endangers its well-being. After protracted discussions and action at Supreme Court level, the re-wilding project won the day. It was clear that Li and colleagues had their work cut out on a number of fronts.

The tiger population in Africa reached fourteen, three were lost and eleven have survived. Out of the eleven, two were hand-reared, and the remaining nine were reared by the mother to thrive in natural conditions. Though they lost two cubs, it has to be acknowledged that nine out of ten South China Tiger cubs died in the zoo bred tiger population in 1990s. The larger project (grand plan) is still waiting for suitable natural habitat in China: the tigers are ready to return and the tide of professional (previously negatively and often hostile) opinion seems to ebbing back to re-visit Li's vision.

A critical question centres on whether the end justifies the means in this example of wildlife preservation in both the growth of wild tigers and available natural habitat in China. The means undoubtedly carried a degree of risk e.g. death of the cubs from an already limited stock in China, the possible introduction of pathogens and viruses (carried both ways) to South Africa and even the potential failure of the 're-wilded' tigers to adapt to Chinese habitat on subsequent reintroduction. No small wonder then that Li's vision came under hefty and sustained critique.

But what if the end goal is achieved: the Chinese government (notably Wildlife Division of China's State Forestry Administration and the National Development and Reform Committee (the all-powerful NDRC)) is spurred into action by providing an appropriate wildlife reservation in the short term and into a longer term plan for the sustained protection for the wild tiger to thrive. By good luck, one might add, there was no serious outbreak of pathogen in the local wildlife in Africa. The tigers looked normal (actually extremely healthy looking compared to any animals, zoo or wild) healthy specimens which in turn started to breed naturally. Only history will tell us the full story.

Many see Li as a maverick, simply as an opportunist with considerable financial resources, undoubted passion but mis-guided, having little (scientific) sense. She has exhibited classic entrepreneurial skills of determination, huge investment in terms of time and money (personal savings) and perseverance in pursuit of her long term goal. She also learned as the project progressed – gathering skills and knowledge when the project needed to (her account of the initial attempts on coaxing the tigers to eat feathered skin carcasses is just one example). She didn't take no for an answer but instead increased her resolve to stay the course. In a BBC radio programme she remarked: "It is impossible to get everyone to agree…nothing was going to be done; you do what you believe in. I don't have a PhD, I don't endeavour to gain one…there is nothing they can do to stop me."[7]

She is well-motivated in that she wants the South China tiger to thrive and ethical in her actions (she does not want to intentionally harm). Also, to be fair to Li and colleagues: they publish all comments which are critical to the programme on the Save China's tigers website.

Incidentally, the word maverick takes its origin from one Samuel A Maverick, a Texas rancher who did not brand his cattle. In the end, Li may not want to see any wild tigers in China branded as such, but simply that they exist and thrive, in good numbers, in the wild for the benefit of the animals themselves and for future generations of mankind.

Help us save the
South China Tiger

4

Potato peels:
a dressing of choice?

Here is an example of an odd-coupling that didn't quite work but one I am sure will capture your imagination: it concerns the application of a characteristic of a food source (potato) and the treatment of a very painful and disfiguring condition in humans – heat or chemical induced burns. One thing you probably didn't know was that in October 2007, the United Nations declared 2008 as the Year of the Potato presumably because of the importance of this crop as a staple food in human nutrition.

Although the potato (Solanum tuberosum) or spud as its more common name contains eighty three per cent water, they are a rich source of dietary energy due to their carbohydrate levels, some protein, organic nutrients e.g. vitamin C and some B vitamins and some nine thousand phenolic compounds which make up a protective chemical defence system for the tuber[1]. Some analysts estimate in processed products between forty and fifty per cent of potatoes end up as waste. Peels are the major portion of processing waste and actually present a major problem in disposal; they are also known to be a rich source of phenolic antioxidants and have been demonstrated to significantly reduce plasma glucose levels in laboratory animals and to ameliorate antioxidative stress.[2,3,4]

In the traditional medicine of Europe, raw potatoes are used for gastrointestinal disorders and topical potato preparations as a hot pack for pain or for softening furuncles. We know that a dry wound is very painful and takes longer to heal; burn patients lose a lot of water through evaporation from the wound and the wounds themselves are liable to become infected. If you press a potato very hard, no moisture comes through the peel owing to its high molecular cell wall components. It's been known that potato peels do not desiccate quickly and provide moisture but someone, somewhere (probably in India) came up with the original idea of applying them to treat burns.

Potato peels prevent quick evaporation and in some instances skin replacement has been found to be quicker when potato peel bandages are used. It was also thought that they had anti-bacterial properties that help in healing burn injuries. In 1990, Keswani and colleagues undertook an observational study of patients in Bombay, comparing burn wounds covered with either boiled potato peels affixed to gauze bandages or gauze dressings alone and found that the application of the potato peel dressing reduced or eliminated desiccation, permitted the survival of superficial skin cells and hastened epithelial regeneration - the outer skin 'wall'[5]. He and his fellow researchers concluded that the simplicity of the preparation of this dressing, the ease of sterilization and its low cost of production make this the dressing of choice for burn wounds. More rigorous bacteriological studies however showed that the potato peels had no intrinsic antibacterial activity, the wounds beneath both dressings (potato v gauze) showing either no growth or, on most occasions, the same bacterial species.

Subrahmanyam undertook a randomised controlled trial of one hundred patients to compare potato skins and honey as a dressing to treat burns.[6] Subjective evidence of relief of pain was comparable, but potato peels were in fact inferior to honey with respect to wound healing time and antibacterial activity. Two more recent systematic reviews of the literature concluded that where sterile potato peel dressings are used, the value of potato peel seems to be in reducing desiccation and thereby promoting healing during the burn recovery phase; there is little evidence of independent antibacterial effect.[7,8]

We might rightly conclude from the evidence (or lack of) that potato peels as they stand don't have much of a future as the dressing of choice in the treatment of burns. From a more entrepreneurial standpoint we might find that perhaps a chemist working in the health-related R&D lab gets to hear of this innovative application and decides to mimic the potato skin structure and produce a sterile substrate that can hold the necessary (sterile) organic compounds which aid healing. Or alternatively, it might lead another microbiologist to examine further the molecular cell wall of the potato and redefine what cellular properties may be of potential use in this area of burn treatment in the future. The connection (bisociation) has been made between two resources: bandaging for burns and high molecular cell wall of the common garden spud or Solanum tuberosum. Equally, an alternative spin-off in relation to sustainability might be in the more efficient and environmentally favourable extraction methods of harnessing the known target compounds from what is still a large waste residue.

The research on skin graft is expanding rapidly particularly in the use of skin substitutes. In addition to survival the current focus in burn care is on improving the long term function and appearance of the healed or replaced skin cover as well as quality of life. This focus on quality has generated a significant interest in the use of skin substitutes to be used to improve wound healing, to control pain, to more rapidly close a burn wound, to improve functional and cosmetic outcome, and, in the case of massive burn area, to increase survival. To more effectively address these new roles, the new generation of skin substitutes is biologically active. The bioactivity can modulate the burn wound instead of just covering the wound. The new products have not yet displaced the more inert standard burn wound dressings but rather are used in conjunction and for quite specific indications.[9]

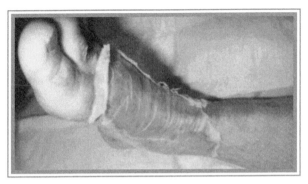

A biologically active flexible burn dressing

5

A tale of alarming mustard
– Japanese style

In 1991 an American writer by the name of Marc Abrahams came up with the novel idea of a way of rewarding scientific research that amused the reader by instigating annual awards entitled 'Ig Nobel'. These are international awards that "honour achievements that first make people laugh, and then make them think". In part, it is a celebration of eccentricity in which the two countries of Britain and Japan have done particularly well. Indeed, Britain was once viewed as a nation of garden-shed engineers or innovators – dismantling engine parts, fixing them, putting together or adapting existing parts to 'improve' the performance or function of the existing product[1]. The fact that many men had a vice in the garden shed would now attract a different puerile response from today's media. But I digress from the main story: a tale of using the rather obnoxious properties of strong mustard in an entirely novel and alarming fashion. The mustard in question is the green Japanese wasabi (you will probably find a small blob of it in a sushi 'meal to go'). The application of this food source was to win the accolade of Ig Nobel for its inventors[2]. But first a short discourse on the chemistry of the substance in question.

This food source contains an active ingredient known to chemists as AIT (Allyl isothiocyanate) a powerful substance which delivers a stinging sensation to the mucus in your nose and upper airway. In contrast to olfactory processing, somatosensory processing helpfully persists during sleep; in other words it is not the smell of the mustard but the effect on the inner membranes of the nose and upper breathing airways which is causing the alarm or stress to the human system.

In 2002 Karin Matsumori, an acquired deaf person, took the basic idea of an odour alarm to a pharmaceutical R&D based company based in Tokyo[3]; she had identified a hidden need. The proportion of the elderly among fire victims is nearly fifty per cent and the mortality rate in the normal sleep range is three times higher than that of other times. The elderly suffer from a deteriorating loss of hearing and she thought that this may be a principal cause in relation to mortality. She was acutely aware that standard household smoke alarms worked on sound alerts; deaf people need a viable alternative.

The researchers were faced with two problems: identifying the odour and the mechanisms for its projection. In the case of the former, they worked on an estimated hundred substances including hydrogen sulphide (rotten eggs). They decided that the best substance for the job was wasabi. On the mechanism side, design technologist at the R&D company had then to find or invent a technology based on an aerosol spray to ensure that it was capable of 'firing' a known concentration of the odorant a predetermined distance (i.e. from the firing cylinder to the person asleep). It was estimated that the firing cylinder had to project a sample of odorant (AIT) in the range 5 -20 ppm at least one metre. Design technology was called for.

The efficacy studies (does the odourant work on sleeping deaf subjects) were formally carried out by Professor Makoto Imai of Shiga University of Medical Science in Japan. Professor Imai is a clinical psychiatrist researching sleep medicine and interested in functional organization of central nervous system. He found that deaf subjects responded more quickly than hearing controls in sleep stage 2 with their mean latencies of approximately 21 sec and 45 sec, respectively. One of his studies looked at response and harmful effect among thirty-one deaf subjects; he noted: tears (three subjects), cough (one subject), pain in nasal cavity (one subject) and sore throat (one subject). Thankfully, these symptoms did not persist[4].

A quick response to AIT (the pungent compound of wasabi) observed in deaf subjects in the study might be a result of lifelong deprivation of auditory stimuli. His work focused on whether the pungent sensation would be processed in the temporal area in the brain that corresponds to original auditory area in deaf subjects. Rather surprisingly, reorganization of brain stimuli may occur not only to people with congenital deafness but also to acquired deafness.[5]

These alarms can now be bought for 50000JPY (approximately three hundred and ninety pounds), but with the possibility of mass production this figure would drop dramatically. The general effectiveness of the alarm 'kit' might be enhanced if deaf people are provided a small 'tester' pack' so that the brain remembers and associates the sensation with the recall of alarm (impending fire and risk to life and limb); this might prove more difficult from a cultural perspective for the Japanese than it seems as wasabi is a favoured 'spice'.

The team of entrepreneurs experimented with many possibilities before opting for wasabi. It took a considerable time and effort of a broad team of people to bring this idea to market. From the identification of need, to the chemists who honed in on wasabi, to the technology designers in the R&D company, through to testing the efficacy and effectiveness in clinical trials and then manufacturing and bringing the product to market. Part of the team effort and acknowledgment should also extend to the deaf people who took part in the clinical trial – their participation has helped bring this idea to a marketable product[6].

By virtue of trial and experience (the entrepreneur's way or creed), there are perhaps three avenues to pursue in future enterprise. First, through further technical design improve the effectiveness of the product: it simply works better with deaf people. Second, try another route to produce the most effective method on the market (there is clearly a market gap or failure). Third, as an unintended consequence of this work, move to a related field of safety where a solution is still to be found e.g. a close tie between the University and the R&D company would approach a new portfolio of as yet unmet need.

The Wasabi Smoke Detector

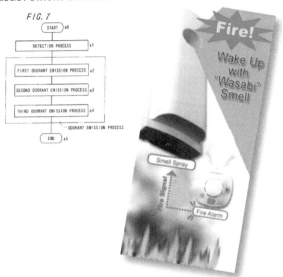

FIG. 7

START a0

DETECTION PROCESS a1

FIRST ODORANT EMISSION PROCESS a2

SECOND ODORANT EMISSION PROCESS a3

THIRD ODORANT EMISSION PROCESS a4

ODORANT EMISSION PROCESS

END a5

Fire!

Wake Up with "Wasabi" Smell

Smell Spray

Fire Signal

Fire Alarm

6

Flow straighteners:
delivering the dose

Asthma is a chronic disease characterized by recurrent attacks of breathlessness and wheezing, which vary in severity and frequency from person to person. Symptoms may occur several times in a day or week in affected individuals, and for some people become worse during physical activity or at night. Recurrent asthma symptoms frequently cause sleeplessness, daytime fatigue, reduced activity levels and school and work absenteeism.

It is estimated that 235 million people currently suffer from asthma; it is the most common chronic disease among children. The World Health Organisation views asthma as a public health problem not just for high-income countries as it occurs in all countries regardless of the level of development.[1] Medication can control asthma; avoiding asthma triggers can also reduce the severity of asthma. Appropriate management of asthma can enable people to enjoy a good quality of life.

During an asthma attack, the lining of the bronchial tubes swell, causing the airways to narrow and reducing the flow of air into and out of the lungs. So we need a little bit of the science to understand the direction of research and development – you need to know the difference between your MDIs from your DPIs. Metered-dose inhalers (MDIs) have grown in popularity since their introduction in the late 1950's and they are currently used by over 25 million Americans for a variety of diseases, such as asthma, chronic obstructive pulmonary disease (COPD), and other lung diseases characterized by obstruction of airflow and shortness of breath.

Metered-dose inhaler products contain therapeutically active ingredients dissolved or suspended in a propellant or a mixture of solvents in compact pressurized aerosol dispensers. Current designs of pre-metered and device-metered DPIs (dry power inhalers), can be driven by patient inspiration alone or with power-assistance of some type. Pre-metered DPIs contain previously measured doses or dose fractions in some type of units (e.g., single or multiple presentations in blisters, capsules, or other cavities) that are subsequently inserted into the device during manufacture or by the patient before use. Thereafter, the dose may be inhaled directly from the pre-metered unit or it may be transferred to a chamber before being inhaled by the patient.[2]

It is fair to say that a huge amount of scientific and engineering R&D has gone into this field of health care. Whilst the patent for the first type of DPI can be traced back to 1864, the first "breath" triggered inhaler didn't come on to the market until 2001; this was followed some ten years later (i.e. the present) when a high performance multi dose DPI unit became available to the public.[3] Interspersed in this timeline is the appearance of a spinhaler in 1967 and this is where our story picks up: how did the idea of a spinning element in an inhaler come to feature in the development of a DPI.

Enter Roger Altounyan a medical doctor, spitfire pilot and bomber instructor who also suffered from asthma. He experimented on two levels: trying to identify an effective drug and in its delivery mode. In the former case through a process of trial and error and by subjecting himself to daily routines of Middle Eastern folk remedy khella: how did it work and could it be the source of a new synthetic asthma drug. Roger tested on himself over two hundred compounds found in khellin. Taking each one, he exposed himself to an extract of guinea pig hair to which he was allergic, and tested his lung function with a spirometer.

Roger discovered in 1965 that khella's active ingredient was khellin. He eventually produced, after some six hundred and seventy tests and trails, a safer chemical based on khellin, sodium cromoglycate. This was later marketed as Intal by Fisons UK. Sodium cromoglycate was the first clinically utilized mast cell stabalizer. The mast cell plays a key role in allergic and asthmatic inflammation. Mast cells contain powerful inflammatory mediators which when released lead to inflammation and bronchoconstriction of the airway. Sodium cromoglycate stabalizes the mast cell thereby preventing the release of the mediators.

Whilst the account of his experimentation to identify a stabiliser for mast cell (inflammatory mediator role) is worthy to be re-told, it is his experimentation on the mode of drug delivery, I want to highlight. Using the front room of his house, Roger designed and experimented for over a period of several months with a small propeller-like mechanism for dry powder delivery.

'One day he noticed that when he sucked one of the models it vibrated and buzzed like a dentist's drill, presumably because the bearing was poor and rattled. Then he wondered if this shaking might prevent the powder from impacting. He tried it with some powder, and at last it produced a steady and efficient inhalation. Ironically, it was the very fault in the eccentric action of the slightly imperfect bearing that made the little machine work. His flying experience is said to be the inspiration for the "spinhaler", a propeller-driven device to deliver sodium cromoglycate deep into the lungs.[4]

By 2007, the same problem (or more accurately two dimensions of the same problem) was still confronting developers: how to get as much of the drug dose into the inner recesses of the lung. A medical devices company based in India teamed up with the design expertise and know-how of a company in Cambridge UK. Over a period of five years (it normally takes up to half that time again) of product development, clinical trials, 'tooling' and testing, a finished product is now on the market.[5] At the heart of this new product which has no battery power is the application of a miniscule version of a flow straightener device that is normally found in jet engines to enable directed thrust. The design consultants came up with a solution which ensured that not only each dose was 'spun' out but guide the drug straight down the throat, leaving the carrier solution (lactose) in the throat. So over time, the ideas in odd-coupling went from single propeller to a jet engine component to come to the aid of producing a highly effective DPI.

The global market for inhalers is estimated to be in the order of 30 billion dollars. A simple low cost nifty device (called the inhaler trainer) has been designed to teach patients how to inhale properly. Shaped like a normal metered drug inhaler, this device lets out a constant b flat sound if inhaled correctly but emits a sharp pitched shrill noise if inhaled too strongly.

Roger was a man driven by enquiry and a desire to find solutions for what in his day was a chronic health problem largely ignored by the medical world. His early attempts at pharmaco R&D though proved unsuccessful and a third attempt at pain measurement, which looked promising, was again shelved by his employers.

By chance he was given a free hand to care for chest patients in what was a disused ward in Monsall Hospital, Manchester UK. This facility provided the much need 'laboratory' to test out his ideas. It was reported that he was so attentive to his patients that those who found difficulty walking could rely on the good doctor to drive them to their bus-stops!

His biographer stated: 'He achieved success through an exceptional combination of sterling qualities: determination not to be distracted by set-backs, whether personal or technical, an infectious enthusiasm…selfless devotion to try out new forms of drugs on himself again and again…his steady determination to make some of his medical colleagues see reason and abandon long-held preconceptions. The whole impetus of his adult life was directed to the service of his fellows.'[6]

It may be coincidence that the latest development of the central mechanistic device contained in a DPI takes its provenance from flight power. Whether this latest development is a coincidence or not, the entrepreneurial and enterprising endeavours of Roger Altounyan merit a place in our Hall of Fame.

The Abbott Inhaler 1948
- the first DPI aerohalor

7

Making materials stick:
the power and necessity of re-creation

(ordinary bathroom sealant)

(ordinary wood shavings)

In a book by Janine Benyus on the ability of nature to inspire us towards innovations, she describes the prodigious outpourings of research from a Materials Research Society annual conference, where three thousand five hundred academics congress to share the fruits of their investigations.[1] Materials are entirely apposite for this next section, as you will later see, with material science 'literally touching everything we touch; every object we walk on, ride in, put on, or pour from is made of a material or several different materials'. This is the unsung world of shatter resistance, tensile strength and surface chemistry. Our progress has been characterised by the ability to harvest, transform and mould new materials: Stone Age, Bronze Age, Iron Age, Oil/ Plastics Age and more recently perhaps the Silicon Age. The new alchemy works under the principle of 'heat, beat and treat'; she notes that it is the way we synthesise just about everything we now produce. Nature, however, does not follow this strategy – its first 'trick of the trade' is to manufacture materials under life friendly conditions – in water or air, at room temperature. Nature is characterised by the lack of high temperatures or toxic chemicals. We won't need a university degree in chemistry to get through this section but it might help to say that researchers split themselves into two groups: inorganic (the hard materials) and organic (the soft materials).

The abalone shell is roughly 3,000 times more fracture resistant than a single crystal of calcium carbonate, the mineral that makes up most of its bulk. It has an inner shell which is two times as strong as any ceramic we can produce; it is a shell that is produced in water and at sea temperature.[2] Most people eat the meat of the abalone and sell the shell; inorganic chemists use them to learn and be amazed by how the shell can be created. The shell displays an intricate crystal architecture involving hexagonal discs of calcium carbonate (chalk) stacked in a brick-wall structure; between each layer of brick is a narrow skin of polymer which acts like a flexible ligament allowing the whole shell to withstand the stress and strains (and possible attack by predators) of sea life. From a range of organic materials that life has created (blood vessels, silk, skin, cellulose) I want to bring to your attention the bivalve Mytilus edulis or more simply known as the mussel. The mussel can extend hundreds of tiny translucent threads or filaments which enable it to filter feed in a tidal zone by sticking itself to any stationary object in the sea bottom or just below the surface in the case of a buoy. By a series of complicated chemical (protein sealants) and physical (vacuum cleaning) reactions the mussel is able to stick to materials in one of the harshest environments known to man.[3] The subject of this odd-coupling is a new material that is strong, malleable, flexible and sticky.

When Jane ni Dhulchaointigh started her design course at the London Royal College of Art (RCA) in 2003, she had no inkling of what she was to create and produce over the next decade in the world of inorganic materials; an inorganic material that would change the culture of not only repairing things but help to revive our innate ability to re-create and improve the functioning of an infinite array of objects.

Jane was a sculptor by craft (and degree) but decided to make the transition from fine art to product design at the RCA, a more linear thinking and product oriented course. She had been experimenting with a large and somewhat random selection of materials; then she focused on two central components namely that of bathroom sealant (sticky silicone) and wood shavings. She produced a basic product: something which could both be moulded and then set, but remained rubbery. It was very basic but the idea was, pardon the pun, cemented in her brain. The idea and its potential application captivated her for the next year.

Serendipity or happenchance was to play a hand in the concept of this new material. In the early days, most of the experimentation was done in her house. When she made up a new batch of product, she realised that she had a limited time to work within owing to the variable setting times. Her partner was to obliquely remark that perhaps the onus was not on her to devise its unique range of functions but rather let other people create what uses the product could be put to. The application of the idea was now duly set (I will stop the punning from herein); the product was literally to tap people's innate creativity to provide solutions that they needed.

The odd-coupling was therefore at two levels not only in the recombining of two materials but also in the attempt to couple the element of function with the element of play. In the latter case the element of play was to adopt a new term by way of 'hacking' (repairing, extending and adapting existing objects and materials).

The air curing rubber's patented technology is unique in its combination of malleability, self-adhesion and flexibility when cured. It feels like modelling clay, and does not require technical instructional manual to use. Once it is cured at room temperature, its durable properties mean that it can be applied on a vast array of materials (cloth, metal, plastic) and it's reliable in more extreme environments 'from the dishwasher to the ocean to Antarctica'.

There now exists an extensive gallery of growing applications (making things better through hacking) of this new material; the gallery will no doubt continue to grow. The author had a go and succeeding at customizing the handles of a pair of skipping ropes.[4]

Apart from the demanding continual cycle of improving the qualities of the product (i.e. the technology platform), future applications for the company involves developing customised handles for sports people in the world of fencing and archery; this work aims to improve grip and thereby both reduce strain and increase power. Other work is being picked up in small scale R&D labs around the country.

By hacking (extending the life of) existing objects and applications, we lower the overall use of greenhouse gases and indeed new production costs. It is also greener by way of not contributing to waste and land re-fill activity.

Her initial interest and skill developed in painting and drawing; this was to develop in the art and skill of being a sculptor. By bringing together hand and brain in a direct way, the ability, confidence and desire to play with new materials was promoted. Perhaps the definition of a sculptor is an 'artistic engineer'.

The need for perseverance, determination and 'listening to the inner self' was ably demonstrated by Jane from the initial idea, to early sketches, fledging company and then in time, through to having an international profile and business. Her take on risk is once again characteristic of entrepreneurs: she never considered it as being a risky process – more a process of making increasingly larger incremental steps and decisions. The risk was to herself (and perhaps to relationship(s)) by the sheer length of time to devote to the 'business' and counter-intuitively by not making a go of it. However, at the end of the day she remarked "we would come out of it the other end… with invaluable experience". She had the foresight to build a strong small team and to off-source a technical problem to an external laboratory. Although, in the latter case, this proved to be less successful in terms of expected outcome and so brought the problem back to the team to work on and solve.

In a smart move to gain a higher profile she sent a batch of the material to a newspaper journalist who critiqued and promoted innovations. It is a smart move if you know that your product or service is good; the opposite could happen if it did not live up to expectations. But Jane and colleagues knew from an early stage that not only was the product sound but that there was a large potential market out there.[5]

In the world of mass production, everything is made to a pre-set range of parameters: XS,S,M,L & XL or more simply child/junior and adult. The new material fills the gap between this mode of mass-production: you can customise objects to your specific size and function. Size, feel and look are now personalised.

What remains on the horizon for Jane and colleagues is to push forward the concept and culture of re-creation and repair. How many times have you heard the refrain that the cost of a new machine or object is almost the cost of a new one..."So, we bin the old one"; there is likely however to have been a considerable energy cost in the initial production. So Jane and colleagues are pushing for large scale cultural and behavioural change in both the repair of faulty/broken objects and in the infinite array of customised small-scale inventions by you and me. Power to your elbow!

The future needs fixing

8

A featherbed frame
– creating a classic mount

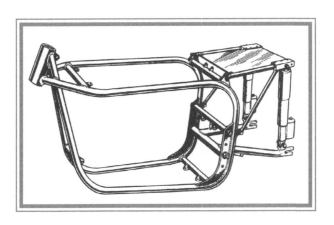

After some anticipation of looking forward to a second-hand book via Amazon, I was at first disappointed by what looked like a thin comic-like booklet. The work was by Gordon Small entitled 'Sweet Dreams – the life and works of Rex McCandless'.[1] This first impression however quickly gave way to one of excitement, awe and respect for what was the work of a genius from Hillsborough, Northern Ireland.

There are some striking similarities between Rex McCandless and Mathew Boulton (see chapter 15) in the way they solved engineering problems. Whatever task or challenge he took on, he came up with a workable solution: motorbikes, racing cars, four wheel drive cross country jeeps, brick manufacture (yes, I have checked) and last but not least autogyros. But it is his work on motorbikes that not only his skills but his true genius was confirmed.

Looking at his early years, I saw a fairly similar pattern in many entrepreneurs: little formal education at senior school level but having self-belief and a willingness to work hard. Rex left school at the young age of thirteen in 1928 to be a general labourer in a flour mill. His various jobs were merely a means to get his hands on what was his growing interest: motorbikes. He learned his craft (mechanics) by servicing lorries which delivered the Daily Herald to London railway stations.

He returned to Northern Ireland to work at Short Brothers and Harland fitting out brakes on Bristol Bombays. He and his younger brother Crombie were soon to gain a strong reputation and build a good business for fixing and repairing any machines; they were once asked to fix a giant bulldozer with nothing but common sense and sheer engineering ability as there were no manuals for reference. Their reputation for high quality repairs soon flourished.

He learned and honed his craft by racing bikes to get a 'feel' for how they work under test conditions. By all accounts he was a good rider as was his younger brother. It was his second bike, the Triumph Tiger 100, which probably gave him the greatest impetus to experiment. It is said that this bike needed a lot of driver effort and concentration: 'sometimes it felt as if the bike was in charge'. Taking up the story in his own words "I fiddled about with it and it was good enough to take the Irish 500 road race championship, held in 1940 at Phoenix Park Dublin and also the hill climb championship'. No mean feat for a self-taught engineer. He recalls

"I never had any formal training. I came to believe that it stops people thinking for themselves. I read many books on technical subjects, but always regarded that as second-hand knowledge. I did my best working in my own way".[2]

By now he knew his craft: rigidity of the frame was critical for wheel alignment (the bike must stay in line with the direction that the driver steers it (irrespective of bend or bump) and secondly the wheel should stay in contact with the road hence the necessity for soft suspension (consistent 'damping' was required). He experimented again with the Tiger 100 by removing a couple of heavy items on the front wheel namely the mudguard and a headlight – the bike then steered much better. Rex built his own machine based on the rigid double loop frame where everything on it was adjustable: the featherbed frame was born. He then built a bike using this frame, adding a swinging arm with vertical hydraulic shock absorbers from a Citroen car and named it the Benial or beast. At that same time, the prestigious Norton Motorcycle Company dismayed at poor track records, went in the opposite direction, intent on building heavier and stronger frames. Norton frames (known as garden gates) were indeed up to sixty pounds heavier than the featherbed and liable to fractures. The photograph below shows Rex on the 'Benial' at the Bangor castle race in 1945; he was to remark that it was the best handling bike he ever drove or raced. By the 1950s, Norton begrudgingly acquiesced and asked Rex to come over to England to build the feather bed frames for racing Norton Bikes.

The featherbed frame was then further developed by Norton to improve the performance of their racing motorcycles around the twisting and demanding Isle of Man TT course in the 1950s. It was later adopted for Norton production motorcycles and is also widely used by motorcyclists on custom built hybrids and cafe racers such as the Triton. The frame became legendary and remains influential to this day.

Rex's upbringing may have had a profound influence in shaping his determination to do something with his life. At the age of twelve, his father gambled on the stock exchange and only succeeded in losing house and home; even more disheartening was the fact that his father left the family home ('skinned out' as the expression was then).

Hi first bike was actually a gift from an auntie who presented him with a 1923 side valve Raleigh – this gift could not have been by pure accident and was probably an extremely fortuitous act that set him on his way to developing a positive interest, creating a business and leaving a legacy.

He was to display a classic entrepreneurial attribute: an unlike or unwillingness to work for someone else. In the late 50s, he was offered a directorship with Ferguson Ltd in Ulster to develop a four wheeled jeep known as 'The Mule'. It had great potential but unfortunately the whole project was to collapse into acrimony with the company putting a lid on any development and not allowing any other R&D on the prototype. As they say entrepreneurship is a risky business – it is telling that Harry Ferguson offered a directorship but not a partnership in the business to develop 'The Mule'.

Like many entrepreneurs, he was imbued with confidence and remarkable self-belief. In his later years of creativity and innovation, his thoughts turned to the design and production of autogyros. The Air Registration Board however was to place strict conditions on flights owing to the severity of accidents. Not put off, Rex built his own ground rig to test out the autogyros and discovered what was causing the fatal accidents. Rex presented his findings to the Board but it was reluctant to lift the constraints on flight access. He experimented, built, tested and flew. That was his way.

He had the chance of expanding his interest into manufacturing of bikes which would then have been fairly lucrative and would have given Norton or BSA a run for its money. His interest wasn't there – it was on the next problem or challenge and not about maximising profit.

In the 1950s, Stanley Wood was reported as saying ' the average motor cyclist had no idea of the debt owed to Rex McCandless…his frame set the standards of road-holding and steering which, forty years on, have yet be bettered'.[3]

'The Beast' with classic featherbed frame

9

Bagging a defence:
a flat-pack solution

It is reported that James (Jimi) William Heselden grew up on a deprived council estate in Yorkshire, left school at fifteen without any formal qualifications and headed 'down the pit'. Mining in the mid-sixties was still a life of fairly tough employment and indeed employment prospects.[1] He lost his job in the wave of pit closures and redundancies that followed the mid-eighties miners' strike. He took what little money he had and set up a sandblasting business.

It seems that he had a good knowledge of geology and soil science. His thoughts turned to reviving an Italian Renaissance invention known as gabions. The word gabion is a French word derived from the Italian word "gabbia" meaning cage. The very early use of these products was by the Chinese who made wicker baskets that were rock-filled for protection of structures against river erosion. In the latter part of the 16th Century the French and British developed similar structures that were soil-filled for personal protection emplacements in military installations. The word gabion was adopted by the French to mean "a fortified position".[2]

In the late 19th century simple wire mesh baskets were being made that could be rock filled and that could provide more permanent solutions to problems of erosion protection in river works and simple earth retaining structures. Greater levels of sophistication in steel wire coating and manufacturing techniques were employed during the latter part of the 20th century. This was combined with significant research being undertaken to understand the performance characteristics of the modern day gabion products. Today, the use of rock-filled gabion products are well accepted techniques in earth protection and earth retaining structures around the world.

Heselden's idea, patented in 1989, was to make them out of galvanised steel, flat-pack them and call them bastions; they were practically impenetrable when filled with earth, stones, water and sand. These barriers were effective and could be erected in one tenth the time it takes to erect an equivalent sandbag barrier. The manufactured portable wire cages ('concertainers') can be filled with earth and sand were originally sold to water companies to shore up the sides of canals, to hold back coastal erosion and to counter flood control on beaches. But Jimi's story doesn't here; if it did, it would not have found a place in a book on odd-coupling. Luck played a helping hand.

By chance, an employee in the procurement office in the Ministry of Defence came to hear of these portable barriers and in their possible application as a defence barrier in another context – in a conflict or a war zone. The barriers were more resilient than traditional sandbags against missiles and mortar attacks. Heselden was subsequently called for interview in London to pitch for a major defence contract. The story goes that he was asked if the company could supply a large number of them by a certain date – he 'inflated' company output production and assured the Ministry that he could meet the contract specifications. When he heard that he had won the contract, he spent a great deal of time making frantic phone calls to family, friends and trusted business acquaintances to help him meet a sizeable contract within the deadline. Entrepreneurs quite often 'sail close to the wind' and depend on business relationships based on trust. The business relationships never failed him and he never failed to meet a business deadline.

The bastions have become standard military equipment for NATO as well as American and British forces. Assembling the bastion entails unfolding it and (if available) using a front end loader to fill it with sand, dirt or gravel. The principle protecting personnel and equipment from enemy fire (or bombs) is very similar to the use of sandbags or earth berms in previous conflicts. The main advantage of the barriers, is the quick and easy setup. Previously, troops had to fill sandbags, a slow undertaking, with one soldier filling about twenty sandbags per hour. Troops using the barriers and a front end loader can do ten times the work of troops using sandbags.

The barriers can be stacked, and they are shipped collapsed in compact sets. Filled with sand, 60 centimetres (24 inches) of barrier thickness will stop rifle bullets and shell fragments. It takes 1.5 metres (five feet) of thickness to prevent penetration by a rocket propelled grenade round. Approximately 1.2 metres (four feet) of thickness provides protection against most car bombs. The boxes were quick and cheap to construct, proving much more effective against mortar attacks than traditional sandbags.

They were used in 2005 to reinforce levees around New Orleans in the few days between Hurricanes Katrina and Rita. During the June 2008 Midwest floods 27,000 feet of barrier wall were shipped to Iowa. In late March 2009, 35,000 feet of barrier were delivered to Fargo, North Dakota to fight floods.

In 2009 Heselden bought the US-based Segway scooter company which makes and distributes the distinctive two-wheeled, self-balancing "gyro" scooters. The purchase of this company is an interesting aside but one which is also critical to the most exciting development in personal transport – v2v or vehicle to vehicle transport. General Motors and BMW are investing in the innovation of urban transport.[3]

The EN-V is GM's vision of what urban cars could look like in the future.[4] Not necessarily its design, since the car's simple structure means it would be very easy to make and fit differently shaped polycarbonate and acrylic bodies to the frame. The EN-V is basically a widened Segway, enclosed in a bubble. This was developed to GM's specifications by the transport technology firm Segway, using gyroscopic and fluid-based levelling sensors to help the vehicle balance whilst on the move. What makes the bubble stand out, however, is the wealth of ideas contained within it; ideas that, if implemented, could change the way we get about. The Segway was clearly not a bad investment from someone who left school with no formal qualifications who then went to labour down a mine shaft.

In 2008 he was awarded an OBE for services to industry and to his philanthropic work. He had donated the best part of £23 million to a charitable Trust in Leeds.[5] When he died in 2010 in what was described as a freak accident, he left a multi-million pound industry behind, dealing with army base defence contracts of on the one hand and major flood defences on the other. He had plans for a range of new models in 2011- Jimi was testing a new model, the cross-country Segway X2, when the fatal accident took place.

He built a highly successful company on the back of technical knowhow; used friends and acquaintances to grow the business and built his business on the basis of trust. He took risks early on with the transition of his business from flood defences to blast defences. He certainly wasn't driven by money and was known for his philanthropic support for social enterprises in Yorkshire and beyond. Jimi has earned himself a place in the Hall of Fame.

10

Arch architecture:
the egg has it

John Kay in his book *Obliquity – why our goals are best achieved indirectly*, recounts the tale of a competition to build the largest dome for the cathedral of Santa Maria del Fiore.[1] Brunelleschi challenged his rivals to a competition: to show how you would balance an egg on a flat piece of marble. His competitors struggled to find a way to achieve what looked like an impossible feat; Brunelleschi tapped the egg down on the marble and thereby rested the egg on the 'broken' end. He went on the eventually solve the problem of designing the dome.

Entrepreneurs develop and master the skill of seeing things differently[2]; a computer can solve a complex specified problem but not so good if we can't really define the problem in the first place. Brunelleschi had the ability to perceive problems differently – so did Will Crawford and Peter Brewin in their design for a 'concrete tent'. Before delving into the work of these two entrepreneurs, we need a short introduction to two contributory factors: architecture and the properties of eggshells.

Arches have been used in structural engineering since ancient times. Arches allow passage through a structure, for example: light through arched windows, or people through arched doorways, or water passing under arched bridges. The Roman aqueduct Pont du Gard, is a classic example.[3] The Pont du Gard was built shortly before the Christian era to allow the aqueduct of Nîmes (which is almost fifty km long) to cross the river Gard. The Roman architects and hydraulic engineers who designed this bridge, which stands almost 50m high and is on three levels (the longest measuring 275 metres) created a technical as well as an artistic masterpiece. The other important feature of the shape of the arch is that it distributes the compressive forces to the weight-bearing piers that support the arch. By the by, you can have fun by asking a kid to grasp an egg between thumb and forefinger (at either apex) and ask them to crush it.

A dome of an eggshell is actually an arch rotated about its vertical axis. Domes are stronger than arches, because of their three-dimensional structure. Arches and domes are both statically stable. The eggshell is strong under compression because a dome has both a horizontal and a vertical component, and so compression applied to any one point is evenly distributed across the dome's surface.

The structure of an eggshell whilst strong in compression is weak in tension. For example, young chicks are not strong, but by exerting tensional forces on the inside of the shell by poking with their beaks, they are able to break out of their shells.

Such dome structures are strong because they can exert horizontal as well as vertical forces to resist compression. This means that great pressure can be applied to an egg's two domes before the shell fractures. As weight is placed on top of the egg, the outer portion of the shell will be subject to compression, while the inner wall of the shell will experience tension. The shell will fracture initially at the inner surface under the point of contact with the weight.

However, the strength of the dome structure of an eggshell is dependent on its geometry, in particular, the radius of curvature. Pointed arches require lower stabilizing forces when subjected to compression than a simple semicircle arch. This means that a highly vaulted dome (low radius of curvature) is stronger than a flatter dome (high radius of curvature).

Crawford and Brewin were undertaking a post-graduate degree at the Royal College of Art in London and decided to enter a competition sponsored by the British Cement Association. The competition was to challenge entrants to come up with new and innovative ways of using concrete. Based on the principle of 'know thy craft', the first challenge they set themselves was to understand the physics and properties of concrete. In the former case it exhibits high compression tendencies and in the latter case it sets with water. What could be simpler? After a great deal of trial and error and a series of prototypes, Crawford and Brewin eventually came up with a form of concrete cloth material.

This achievement then got them to thinking of the ability to create a 'building' which you erect quickly in disaster zones or in areas where housing might not be available. The next challenge was to do this to scale – but what was the market? They visited a number of aid agencies in Uganda to test out the need for such shelters. This experience gave them the confidence to pursue their idea. With the production of a prototype, they were able to win support in the shape of a government grant and the attention of a number of investors. By 2011, they were in production mode utilising the tell-tale shape of an elongated egg-shell dome for the shelter.

Concrete Canvas Shelters are rapidly deployable hardened shelters that require only water and air for construction. One shelter can be deployed by two people without any training in under an hour and is ready to use in only twenty four hours. Essentially, these shelters are inflatable concrete buildings.

It took four years from the first idea to having the first product in production; it required development of not just the technology and product but of all the production machinery. At the start Brewin and Crawford borrowed a factory that was scheduled to be demolished from one of their supplier; they would work from nine in the morning and go for a pint just before eleven - closing time of a pub.

The business is now going from strength to strength, turnover tripled in the last year and they have Concrete Canvas projects in over 40 countries. However, one of the reasons for the success has been flexibility - the vast majority of sales and growth are for the Concrete Canvas material rather than the shelters. They developed this material as nothing like it existed and they needed it to enable the shelter concept to work. The two entrepreneurs are now working on further applications of concrete cloth.

What a concrete tent looks like

11

Crossing on the diagonal:
dangerous habits for children

The next time you are anywhere near a clump of tress, stop a moment and consider how your angle to the clump affects your vision through them. This rather innocuous exercise might have led a young engineer to come up with not only a pedestrian barrier solution that was to save many lives especially those of children but was on a broader scale to contribute to a major debate on what constitutes safety in urban streets.[1]

Doug Stewart having graduated from Aberdeen University in civil and mechanical engineering started off his career in a fairly standard direction. By the mid-sixties he took up a post at Aberdeen County Council in the newly emerging area of traffic engineering; this post led him to accident investigation and prevention (AIP). The area was at that time a new 'science' analysing road accidents, deducing their causes and finding ways to prevent them. He became fascinated in the study of events that bridged or coupled engineering design and human psychology. His job was to rectify accident black-spots for Aberdeen; his studies also revealed the dangers of building bends in the road that are 'transitional spiral' shaped rather than circular; the former has a direct correlation with higher accident rates. It seems that transition spiral curves are safe for trains but not for cars. His research apparently helped to influence the State of California to discontinue the use of transitional spiral bend curvature for roads. But I digress.

Post war guardrails in busy streets were based on the principle of trying to direct pedestrians to relatively safer crossing points. Not much work had been done on reviewing this principle for some thirty years. The dynamic interface between driver and pedestrian had not been studied to any great depth, and it was generally assumed that pedestrian barriers were always beneficial. Thus they were widely used at danger spots (crossings, junctions and schools) where they should, in theory, have saved many accidents. Looking for international differences that might provide explanation, a significant one seemed to be the design and use of guardrails. The standard British pattern comprised closely spaced vertical bars making it difficult to climb over or through, but blocking visibility at the shallow angle required by a driver. In the late seventies the UK had the best record in Europe for driver fatalities but the worst casualty rate for child pedestrians. Of the 22,000 annual accidents approximately 140 pedestrians were killed or injured crossing roads, about half of them children. The challenge was not only the maximisation of pedestrians' safety but excellent driver-to-pedestrian visibility. In the late seventies there was little awareness that lack of visibility through barriers was causing accidents.

Doug started to doodle on the angle and spacing on the vertical bars which in time led to the first real prototype of a radical re-design of a pedestrian guardrail; he called the new design Visirail. An extensive survey in London, however, showed only a 13 per cent fall in accidents after the erection of barriers - and child accidents actually increased. In the summer of 1983 with the co-operation of several local authorities numerous sites were investigated, as in the London survey.[2] Accidents were found to have dropped after the erection of Visirail, for both pedestrians and vehicles, both adults and children. Overall reduction was a remarkable 46 per cent and the most impressive results were where ordinary barriers had been replaced. For comparison the travel and accidents savings of new or improved roads generally take 10 years or more to cover their cost. It was estimated that pay-back period was less than two months and the economic rate of return (ERR) over 700 per cent per year. This should be compared with the Department of Transport's guideline for accident reduction of 50 per cent ERR. Pretty impressive.

Merely by locating the vertical infill bars in zigzag fashion across the plan diagonal each one metre length of rail of the usual "solid" effect of infill bars, when viewed at a slight angle, is virtually eliminated. Indeed the "transparency" of Visirail increases to as much as 77 per cent at a distance of 45m when viewed by a driver 2.5m from the rail. When travelling alongside Visirail the driver, therefore has the impression that it is becoming invisible about 50m ahead- at the point where she most requires to see through-it. The frame construction of Visirail posts makes them as transparent as the panel; so the pedestrian, the small child and the approaching vehicle are all clearly visible to each other.

Apart from its widespread use in the UK, Visirail was also licensed to a major Norwegian company for production in Scandinavia. This successful British invention has reduced the accident rate, helped save many lives (especially children) and is continuing to do so.[3]

Despite being side-lined at work, Doug had the dogged determination to follow his interest and passion in the little researched area of civil engineering, road safety and human psychology. He was to fund his own research on visual illusion to test and confirm a hypothesis that car drivers think that children in the distance are adults; this tendency delays braking and thereby increases risk. He was to conclude: '...our innate judgment of collision is unsuitable for traffic speeds because it is "designed" for human locomotion. It was exciting to find that just a few lines of calculus could reveal how our minds can make the extraordinary computation necessary to catch a cricket ball, for example, yet misjudge distance to child pedestrians'. He exhibited the critical factor of perseverance by undertaking eight years of part –time study to gain a PhD. Although he demonstrated that this driver error occurs in most child pedestrian accidents, his research does not appear to have been developed or applied.

Perhaps the other major contribution the work on pedestrian guardrails has been its contribution to the emergence of a lively debate in urban planning and the concept of shared space; one part of this concept introduces the notion of physically removing barriers and line markings to help to reduce accidents.[4] In a similar vein, experiments have yet to demonstrate that removing line markings in certain roads can lead to a reduction in overall speed by car drivers. Currently there seems to be some evidence for and against the removing of lane markings.[5]

Created by a Dutch engineer Hans Mondermann shared space refers to 'principles of legibility and context' to allow 'traffic to be fully integrated with other human activity, not separated from it'; an example of his work can be seen in the town of Drachten in the Netherlands which has seen road deaths reduced in the town centre.[6] In other words, traffic and pedestrians, young and old, fit and infirm, can share the same road space with limited guidance and separation, such as kerbs and guardrails. Traffic control, moves from a predominance of signs and regulation, to one where there is a need for much stronger eye contact between driver and pedestrian. To prove his point, it is said that Mondermann would walk backwards across a street with his arms folded. The press cottoned on to this idea of stripping away as much 'architecture' from thoroughfares to label the idea as 'naked streets'.[7] On a more formal note, the Department of Civil and Environmental Engineering at Imperial College London is undertaking formal research on the phased introduction of the 'shared space' concept in Exhibition Road in Kensington.[8] The success of this scheme could have a defining influence on city centre planning in all developed countries.

It would be unethical to conduct a randomised controlled trial given the nature of risk to life and limb (especially those of young children). One way to overcome research design anomalies is to carry out simultaneous research on many randomly-selected sites.

The next time you are anywhere near a school crossing with metal barriers, take a look to see if the vertical bars are slanted to ensure that visibility through them remains high (see below); the next time you are strolling down a busy high street check out the pedestrian barriers (or lack of them) and judge for yourself whether vehicles and humans can co-exist in some form of minimised risk harmony.

12

Promoting chips in the health service

– a quiet revolution in improving health care.

Most of the time our wallets and purses become laden with infrequently used plastic cards. We are constantly being asked to take out another loyalty card with the lure of rewards. The most frequent use is of course for financial transactions but more lately they have been used to store any type of data and one of the latest adaptations – the so-called wafer- is little more than a promotional gimmick. However one general practitioner (physician) saw the potential of the data wafer to help bring about a quiet revolution in patient care and rights.

Nestled in the quiet and peaceful country lanes of the small town of Litcham, Norfolk (England) sits an idyllic General Practitioner (GP) medical centre. It would not be the first place to look for state of the art innovation or application of one technology into another setting. You would more expect it to be placed in the new and vibrant high tech centre in London, say in Old Street[1]. But as they say appearances are often deceptive. The background context for this wonderful piece of innovation is in the empowerment of the patient – part of a cultural shift in the UK which moves beyond rhetoric to place the patient at the centre of his or her health care.

Managing complex care is hard. A patient has to schedule appointments with a number of clinicians, manage probably a number of medications and co-ordinate with family and friends who participate in the care. Ten million people in the UK alone have long-term illnesses that need this kind of care, including diabetes, asthma and heart disease.

Over the years, one clinician noticed that his clinical team was relying on him to know important information. This was not because he trained as a doctor, but because he was the only one who turned up to all the appointments! Dr. Mohammad Al-Ubaydli who has a long term condition, realised that information technology could not only support a patient but improve outcomes. He set up a new business, a social enterprise, which gave patients control of their records. He and his team have built a website to give each patient better tools to manage their health. Not surprisingly he named the website and wrote a definitive book on 'patients know best'.[2]

In one of Dr Brown's home visits to patients, he was directed to the fridge containing examples and records of the patient's medication. He quickly realised that this record was simply out of date and presented a safety risk; moreover, ambulance staff called to an emergency in a patient's home would invariably ask for such medical records. He knew that something better was needed and became increasingly frustrated by the lack of access to reliable information. He wanted to have access to something in which all information was in one place. Such experience triggered the idea to couple state of the art information cards to hold patient medical records.

With regards to access to your health records (in England), you do not need to make a formal application. Nothing in the law prevents healthcare professionals from informally showing you your own records.

Electronic patient record (EPR) systems have the potential to bring huge benefits to patients and are being implemented in health systems across the developed world. Storing and sharing health information electronically can speed up clinical communication, reduce the number of errors, and assist doctors in diagnosis and treatment. Patients can have more control of their own healthcare. Electronic data also have vast potential to improve the quality of healthcare audit and research. However, increasing access to data through EPR systems also brings new risks to the privacy and security of health records.[3] This is where it gets slightly more complicated - The main plank of the NHS IT programme will create two separate EPR systems: a national Summary Care Record (SCR), containing basic information, and local Detailed Care Records (DCRs), containing more comprehensive clinical information. The latter is recognised as the 'Holy Grail' as such systems can improve safety and efficiency, support key activities such as prescribing, and vastly increase the effectiveness of clinical communication and allow local organisations to share detailed clinical information. Julian is attempting to deliver part of this Holy Grail.

As the House of Commons Select Committee noted, there is a big but on electronic transfer of medical records and information - a concern for confidentiality of patient information. However, the NHS secure network in England does allow appropriate external agencies to access patient records so long as they meet exacting standards of security – part of which is to encrypt patient information so that only the patient can gain access and to whomsoever the patients grants access. Julian and colleagues have addressed the stringent standards concerning safety and confidentiality.

The emergence of the smart card heralds a pivotal step in enhancing patient empowerment; Julian however did not stop here. He has created a unifying suite of IT software programmes which optimise cost-effective care. It is a technology solution that provides a comprehensive picture of medicines and clinical management. It provides real-time data on admissions and referrals, formulary management, savings from prescribing budgets and accurate data which can be used as a benchmark to compare with over 4000 health centres practices throughout England. What is even more attractive in this proposition is that the data is automatically collated, analysed and presented. In short, what we have here is a prodigious data mining exercise at national scale. Did Julian stop here? No.

One might be forgiven in thinking he had concentrated in trying to maintain a high level 'status quo' – but we are dealing with a person of incredible drive and determination to put things right and to make things (data) work better. Part of the data mining now extends to developing a rich data bank of anonymised patient case scenarios for continuing professional development purposes. Health professionals can now "sit in" and/or contribute to educational discussions with colleagues from around the globe on difficult or perplexing cases.

It turns out that Julian's entrepreneurial flair emerged from the tender age of eleven when he was to place an advert in a local shop to collect unwanted personal computers; this love of computers was to extend to secondary school where he would spend his time busying himself with electronics in the school labs. Later on to cover the costs of studying at medical school he was to tap into his entrepreneurial skills by importing and exporting medical textbooks to India.

On a more psychological level, Julian felt that he was lucky to be brought up in an era that was on the cusp of the 'IT' revolution. He feels that he is in a better position to judge and appraise the true value of existing and emerging developments in information technology. He therefore feels that he is in a good position to evaluate not whether his smart card should work but whether it will work in the future.

When you meet him, you get the sense that Dr Brown is an individual driven by a strong sense of purpose – a desire to make a difference. You witness a person who is happy in his work. He obviously makes a difference at the individual (patient) level but has set himself the task on making a difference on a national scale. Such work brings him into contact with a much larger and diversified network of people with whom he can share ideas and hopes.

He is not driven by financial reward, such rewards in his words are "side-effects"; in fact, any profits from the commercial arm of his companies in effect 'subsidise' the educational oriented initiatives and fund specific R&D work. He is driven by a desire to make things easier and better; he would like to leave a positive legacy in the field of primary care for patients and for professional colleagues.

Looking on the horizon, another strand of his work will see the integration of more hospitals records (e.g. radiology) coming through to become part of the primary care software platform he has created for large complex data sets that not only 'talk' to one another but makes sense of the wealth of data. In his work he promotes the dictum: *'better information, better health, better have it'.*

A smart card for patients

13

Juxtaposition:
an artistic licence in odd-coupling

A simple bouquet of flowers

The definition of graffiti in the Oxford English Dictionary is quoted as: 'writing or drawings scribbled, scratched, or sprayed illicitly on a wall or other surface in a public place.'[1] The usage of the term illicit is interesting as it coveys not only a legal context but also one of moral tone. Graffiti art as you probably know dates back to ancient classical Greece and the Roman Empire.[2] The word is also related to a method of scratching through a layer of paint in order to reveal another pigmented layer below. It is still not clear when exactly the word graffiti was first used to distinguish an art form, though many authors point to the early 1970s. This section of the book looks at juxtaposition as an artistic licence in odd-coupling. Juxtaposition (the notion or act of two things being seen or placed close together with contrasting effect) has been used in a number of art forms and has been used to great effect in graffiti art but let me start with two examples from the world of cinema.

The film *A Clockwork Orange* (1972) adapted from the work of Anthony Burgess's novel of 1962 and jointly directed with Stanley Kubrick, creates a strange dissonance in the mind of the viewer by overlaying classical pieces of music on what are disturbing and graphic images of torture, rape and murder.[3] On a more joyful note, in the film *The Thomas Crown Affair* (1999) directed by John McTiernan, the supposed art thief sets up an elaborate, this time, comic twist to throw off the cack-handed police.[4] Increasing numbers of well-dressed men in bowler hats carrying identical briefcases invade the museum (where the supposed theft took place – not giving the game away if you haven't seen Rene Russo – sorry I mean the movie). In the ensuing confusion, our man can slip the net and 'finish the job'. The police start to arrest the bowler-hatted men and open the brief cases – hundreds of copies of Magritte's surrealist painting *The Son of Man* spill to the floor. This iconic painting juxtapositions an apple in front of the man's face – an elaborate play by Magritte on seeing and being seen.

Graffiti fits the model of entrepreneurship with respect to the utilisation of resources i.e. utilising other people's or organisation's property albeit in an apparent illicit manner. Graffiti art by virtue of its physical locale can also capture the public eye in a very direct and frequent way and therefore has an inbuilt feature of free marketing and promotion.

Part of this section has proved rather difficult to write as the subject is a UK graffiti artist known simply as Banksy. The artist is a little like a modern day 'Lone Ranger' fighting apparent injustices – rides into town (though not on horseback), masked to hide his identity, does a job and then disappears back over the horizon. His work has been described variously as 'cheeky and defiant', embodying 'gallows humour', 'politically more engaged, funnier, more provocative' and of using 'guerrilla tactics'. But I wish to focus on the central theme of odd-coupling in his work rather than early influences which have helped to shape the artist or on his work per se.

One such example is the positioning of a suicide waistcoat on a Greek statue, a statue in which the arms are already missing. Another piece has a Queen's Horse Guard sitting in full splendour of uniform atop a pantomime horse. And yet another has a giant barcode being used to depict the side of the circus trailer to keep wild animals from escaping though the tiger is already out and on the prowl.

He extends this use of odd-coupling by preying on an existing patterns or marks on a wall or road. In one classic example, he uses a thin white line to represent a very long line of heroin at which a member of our constabulary is caught kneeling and about to inhale. He uses this to great effect in visual puns e.g. a girl sliding down an angled drain pipe blowing bubbles. Banksy has this skill of "seeing" an opportunity to re-combine a resource in a different way to convey a different meaning.

There is also the use of unusual locale such as 'Falling rich shopper with trolley' which is located some thirty feet up on an office block wall; this painting includes an accompanying drop shadow of the scene for increasing effect. In '*No loitering, New Orleans*', we have the scenario of an elderly black man in his rocking chair painted on a wall in a desolate run-down part of the neighbourhood; whether in hope or desperation he holds a small star and stripes flag in his hand. In '*Show me the Monet*' we have a re-working of Claude-Oscar Monet's famous painting of 1899 entitled *The Water Lily Pond*, only this time the scene is transformed by an all too familiar sight of ditched supermarket trolleys and the presence of a ubiquitous traffic cone. One of the most striking example of his juxtaposition is the use of a bouquet of flowers in the throwing arm of an (assumed) rioter.

As noted above, this artist keeps himself out of the limelight and so very little is known about him apart from anecdotes from friends and aquaintences. There is however a note on serendipidy in his formative years.[5] The artist recalled an early escape from the hands of the law when spraying graffiti on trains in a depot. Making off, he realised that he had become separated from his fellow artists and decided the best course of action was to lie low in the bowels of a skip (large metal waste bucket). Under the debris of old oil cans and cardboard, he realised that the boards were in fact large stencils; it then clicked – spraying was taking too long to complete, he needed a quicker route to complete his work and stencils would provide such a route. By a strange quirk of fate, stencils are used of course to label pallet crates containing military hardware and ammunition.

He is reported as saying in an interview with *Wired* in 2005, "I always wanted to be a fireman, do something good for the world...to show that money hadnt crushed the humanity out of everything". He was described as 'focused and driven' by a fellow graffiti artist Ghostboy and as 'always having a sense of direction, knowing exactly where he wanted to go'.

In relation to risk, our artist always ran the risk of being apprehended by the police. There was also the notion of his work having a double edged sword: whilst you don't have to pay for the resources of walls (etc), someone can piant over or vandalise (often for territorial reasons).

He was quick to appreciate the skills and benefits of self-publication releasing three books in quick succession (*Banging Your Head against a Brick Wall*, Existencilism, and Cut it Out). His work was therefore not restricted by the physical locale of his art. Known as the little black books, they were released between 2001 and 2004 and were sold at the relatively low price of a few pounds. The books contained examples of his work, 'musings' on life and the methods he used in the art of stencilling.[6]

His work sits outside the art intelligentsia or the art world and his pictures rarely refer to other art or the art world. Indeed, he exhibited true entrepreneurial spirit on a number of occasions by 'donating' and displaying his art, unannounced that is, to various museums in London and New York. On most of these occasions, the museum in question allowed the works to remain in view.

In 2007, owners of a house in Bristol were fortunate to have a Banksy mural on a side wall. In attempting to sell the house, they advertised it as a mural with a house attached. In that same year, A YouGov poll declared the artist as one of the most influential art heroes for the under twenty five age group.

Network Rail in England declared its policy not to remove

any works that could be authenticated as the work of Banksy; other graffitti artists would however be vigourously pursued and charged with criminal behaviour.

Alan Bamberger, a US art consultant and author, felt that his work would not be considered in future years as 'works of art', but I am not sure the artist cares or cared for such accolades. For the moment, his prints and other forms of art now sell for large sums of money.

14

Tearing a strip off carbon:
a bright future for graphene

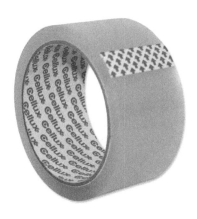

One might be forgiven to think that carbon is a miracle element; it certainly caught the imagination of Primo Levi is his fascinating account of the world of chemistry in *The Periodic Table*.[1] In a way, my final chapter is in a small part, a homage to this author; it wasn't by accident that he placed the chapter on carbon as the finale: 'one must make an exception for carbon, it says everything to everyone...(it is) the element of life'. A form of carbon has been shown to open up huge possibilities in thermal and electronic applications and is the subject of this penultimate chapter.

A pencil's 'lead' is primarily graphite, made up of millions of sheets of graphene. Graphene has remarkable mechanical strength, because the bond that carbon atoms form between themselves is one of the strongest known. Graphene consists of one-atom-thick layers of tightly-packed carbon atoms arranged in hexagons. It is the thinnest and strongest material known to science estimated at 100 times stronger than steel and it conducts electricity better than copper.[2] First discovered in 2004, graphene is a close cousin of carbon nanotubes, which are in effect layers of graphene rolled up.[3] Its incredible mechanical and electronic properties are well known, but it is difficult to make in large quantities.

Extracting feasible samples of graphene remained tricky until two researchers came up with a novel odd-coupling idea. The appearance of a workable sample of graphene owes its provenance to the powerful characteristics of good old household sticky tape. Sticky tape is renowned for its characteristic of holding or binding two materials together; it is not used to pull things apart. Some of us may have used its properties to remove fluff from an item of clothing - but no scientists had ever dreamt of using it in the context of obtaining a resource form of ground breaking applications.

Andre Geim and Konstantin Novoselov of Manchester University (UK) were working in the field of *mesoscopic* physics - a sub-discipline of condensed matter physics which deals with materials of an intermediate length scale.[4] The scale of such materials can be described as being between the size of a quantity of atoms (such as a molecule) and of materials measuring micrometres. They placed adhesive tape on graphite and started to 'tear' off thin flakes of carbon. In the beginning they managed to accumulate many layers of graphite. They then folded the tape in half and stuck it to the existing tape and split them again; the procedure was repeated many times. At each successive tear, the flakes spilt into ever thinner flakes of graphite. They were left with very thin flakes which were dissolved into a solution. The breakthrough was the finding that the thin flakes were in fact stable, moreover they did not lump together or re-combine in solution. The potential of this application e.g. in the making of a transistor, was realised.

Geim and Novoselov were then to transfer the layers of graphite to a plate layered with oxidised silicon. Using microscopy techniques, the researchers were able to determine the actual number of graphene layers in the sample. Geim and Novoselov were awarded the Nobel Prize in Physics for this breakthrough.

Transistors made from such samples have been shown to operate at gigahertz frequencies - comparable to the speed of modern computers. The material could theoretically operate near terahertz frequencies, hundreds of times faster. The electrical properties of graphene make it a prime candidate to replace silicon transistors – the switches that change the flow of current and form the heart of personal computers and mainstream electronics.

The transparent samples can be fixed to any surface and bent or twisted without damaging them. When the technique is perfected, such films could be used in solar cells as well as any number of bendy, thin, transparent gadgetry, such as crystal-clear, flexible displays. For wider application however, graphene must obviously be made in larger sheets while maintaining the high quality of the smaller samples.

A suggestion first proposed a few years ago is now coming to fruition: evaporating a mixture of large carbon-containing molecules and firing it over a heated metal surface. The molecules break down, releasing carbon that re-organise on the surface in neat graphene sheets. The precise conditions of the experiment determine how many sheets are produced.

While growth of such films on metal surfaces has been known to happen for decades, no one had been able to remove the films from the metal, and no one knew if graphene, once removed, would maintain its spectacular potential. Researchers at Sungkyunkwan University in Seoul, South Korea, have applied the technique to produce films of up to 12 sheets on extremely thin pieces of nickel. By dissolving the nickel with chemicals, the researchers were left with graphene films they could stick to a flexible polymer called PET. The researchers went on to show that because the films are so robust, they maintain their striking electronic properties even when bent and twisted. The work confirms that this approach is the most promising path towards bendy, practically invisible electronics.

In 2010, Jing Kong of the Massachusetts Institute of Technology (MIT) published the first account of successfully producing graphene films using the nickel technique. Graphene offers much of the promise of carbon nanotubes, in sheet form. They showed that the precise structure of the graphene films produced could be controlled by putting a nanometre-scale pattern on the thin nickel plates.[5]

In 2012, Yong Chen led a group of researchers from Purdue University, US, that published a paper on the arXiv website detailing a related approach. After production, their films were deposited onto silicon-based substrates, showing a potential means to supplement existing microelectronics with the terrifying speed of graphene components. Yong noted that the samples produced using the new technique are so far relatively disordered and made of regions of differing numbers of graphene layers. [6]

Widespread availability of larger, high-quality graphene films will vastly speed up research into the material's properties, putting researchers ever closer to real applications.

Andre Geim takes up the storyline: "This technique shows the missing element for the whole story, from finding graphene to making real transistors because it shows that industrial scale production is possible....Until now, everyone has been using our so-called 'pencil technique' (the sticky-tape method) but the disadvantage is that the graphite crystals are quite small - it's really painstaking research...It took five years from our demonstration of the beautiful properties of isolated graphene and now, at last, these groups have demonstrated that larger scale production possible." Over two hundred companies and start-ups in the UK are currently involved in research around graphene.[7]

A pencil's 'lead' is primarily graphite, made up of
millions of sheets of graphene
Graphene consists of one-atom-thick layers of
carbon atoms arranged in hexagons

15

Boulton & Watt:
a partnership for the common good

Mathew Boulton

James Watt

To illustrate the broader concept, I will turn to history which has provided us with a striking (pardon the pun) example of odd-coupling. In the Mints of the mid eighteen century, coins were struck by the laborious manual operation of a press (see figure 1). This was a highly labour intensive operation, slow and unfortunately producing coins of relatively poor quality. The Royal Mint, which alone had the privilege of issuing legal tender, confined itself to the production of gold and silver coins. Smaller tender, copper coins, were very scarce and the market gap was met by the local production of tokens where the many taverns would accept and trade. Despite the penalty for counterfeiting, transportation or hanging, it was an open secret that such practices were widespread and accepted. Indeed in the mid eighteenth century it was reckoned that half the copper coinage in England was counterfeit.[1] It was acknowledged that the Birmingham's black market was a hotbed for counterfeiting as the city had a wealth of artists skilled in die sinking and die stamping of toys. The term toys refers to any small intricate

Figure 1: The Art of Coining 1750

workings of metal, usually silver e.g. buckles (which every fashionable gent had on his shoes), walking stick handles, snuff boxes, buttons, pins and base metal nails. Little was being done to rectify this situation and no plans were on the horizon – besides the Royal Mint was not charged with remedying the practice as it did not perceive it was part of the problem. This predicament was to undergo radical appraisal and change and this change was down to one man, Mathew Boulton, a seasoned businessman, scientist, engineer, fine metal worker and entrepreneur. Boulton was born in 1728 to a well-off family and was therefore fortunate to have a decent education. He would recite that he was doubly lucky to be born in 1728 as this was the precise number of cubic inches in a cubic foot. At the tender age of fourteen however he entered his father's business of 'toy' manufacture.

Boulton's first foray into business partnership was a concerted attempt to bridge the twin functions of manufacturer and merchant, to expand upon the scale of his enterprise to foreign markets with a staff that would reach around the seven hundred mark. His work in relation to silver borders (where silver is covered a baser metal) and silver plate was recognised as being of the highest quality in its day. He was feted by royals, the rich and the well to do; they were dined at Soho House in Handsworth Heath (Birmingham) and orders came flooding in from many parts of the globe. By all accounts, work at Soho was a great success but there was one weakness in the infrastructure – in the summer months the availability of water became quite scarce.

Boulton's factory needed a steady and adequate supply of water throughout the year. Enter the skill if not genius of his second partner- a Scot by the name of James Watt, an instrument maker and protégé of Professor Joseph Black of Glasgow University. Watt's invention was to adapt and improve the so-called Newcommen (or atmospheric pump) engine to such effect as to save at least two thirds of coal expenditure. Boulton was quick to seize upon this opportunity and in 1775 after two meetings, a semi- formal partnership between the two was drawn up.[2] Their work was simply prodigious: by 1780 they had erected in situ forty eight pumps in mines to pump out water from ever deeper mineshafts.

Not content with this success, Boulton urged Watt to progress to a rotative engine. After a few prototypes, the first engine was installed in the Albion Flour Mill in London which saw the mill significantly reduced the price of flour in the metropolis – much to the disdain of the smaller flour grinders.

Then came a stroke of odd-coupling genius: apply the rotative engine to the manufacture of coins. Boulton was convinced of the potential of his invention and took out a Letters Patent for them. He was duly granted a patent for the devices on July 8th 1790 (No 1757) under the title "Application of motive power to Stamping and Coining". Boulton explained in the specification: 'The essential parts of this Invention are – First, the applying the power of mills or steam engines to the working presses in place of men's labour, as has hitherto been practised. Secondly, the applying the elastic force of the atmosphere acting upon the piston of an air pump to give the necessary velocity to… strike the blow which coins the money. Thirdly that the arm H which raises the pistons of the air pumps…is totally disengaged from the…fly of the press…during the time the piece F.f acts upon it by which means that bar is allowed to recoil in a natural manner and does not give the shakes which would be occasioned to the whole machine by it vis inertia if it were acted upon immediately…'

This specification is better understood by reference to figure 2. We know that his mind had been vexed by the sorry state of affairs in relation to the quality of coinage and the amount of counterfeit. His idea was to raise the overall quality of coins struck so that it would be difficult to imitate easily; moreover, the intrinsic value of each and every coin should be near to its trading worth. His plans to improve the overall quality of coins fell on deaf ears; his first major contract which was with the East India Company helped to strengthen his vision and resolve. By 1788 he had set up the Soho Mint in Birmingham and had six presses in full operation. Orders came in from the American colonies and from Sierra Leone Company. He was eventually to be given the privilege of producing coinage for the Royal Mint.

Leaving aside the injustices and dangers of child labour, the minting presses were a great success. Here is an account from the Soho Mint, dated 1792: 'Mr Boulton's new machinery works with less friction, less wear, less noise, is less liable to be out of order, and can strike very much more than any apparatus ever before invented; for it is capable of striking at the rate of 26,000 ecus or English crowns, or, 50,000 of half their diameter, in one hour, and of working night and day without fatigue to the boys, provided two sets of them work alternately for ten hours each'.

In producing coins for the Royal Mint, he set in place one criterion for quality, that a defined number of coins would equal an exact length (8 two-penny pieces, placed edge to edge to measure 1 foot). The quality of his work in coinage was matched in his foray into producing high quality medals of state e.g. the Trafalgar Medal which was issued to 'every man who took part no less'. When a new Royal Mint was to be constructed, he was given the honour of overall project management. As the Soho Mint was to supply coinage to the royal mints of Russia, Spain and Denmark a special decreed from the King was required. It read: 'Act to enable Mathew Boulton, engineer, to export the Machinery necessary for erecting a Mint in the dominions of His Imperial Majesty, The Emperor of all Russias.'[3]

He was always experimenting and he acknowledged that many of his ideas did not bear fruit. He was self-driven, constantly trying to improve the quality of the product he was currently working on. By tackling counterfeiting he obviously pursued the potential of a great enterprise but equally Boulton talked about the terrible effects that counterfeit had on a labourer's wage, where parts of it were not legal tender. Moreover, early attempts to persuade the government of the day to tackle counterfeiting were ignored – yet he still persevered. He was seen as the master craftsmen of coin and medal production on an international level; he was also a shrewd businessman and reader of men – he was to place a counter on all coinage presses so that he knew the tally of coins at the end of each day's work (and hence to ensure his products 'did not go out the back door').

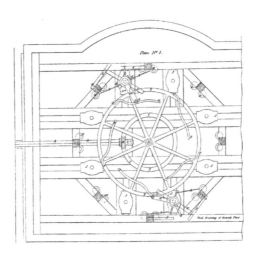

Figure 2

He also took great risks in placing so much of his resources behind steam power – convinced as he was that the benefits of steam driven machines were the future of production. An insight as to his thinking is provided by a letter he wrote to the keeper of a licence for Watts' first prototype (a Mr J Roebuck) who rather too unkindly agreed to a licence for use of the machine in the counties of Warwick, Stafford and Derby. Boulton politely refused stating that he wanted to apply this to make 'for all the world'.

By virtue of his second marriage, he came in time to inherit a small fortune. He chose not to lead the idle life of a gentleman but through dint of hard labour become a 'constant contributor to the purse of the commonwealth'. Boulton would have been very happy for this quote as his epitaph. His portrait would surely grace our Hall of Fame for entrepreneurs.

Epilogue

There are five central tenets in my thinking about entrepreneurship. The first has already been alluded to in that I believe entrepreneurship is about meaningful work, where you create a new type of service or product that helps or improves society in some way – be it in one or more of economic, social, health, cultural, environmental terms. Thus it is not about making money per se though good entrepreneurship will inevitably do so. So, if you are reading this with the intention of boosting your sales to make money, alas you will not find the 'top ten tips' – though hopefully you still might have found it a very good read nevertheless. As an aside, the purpose of writing this book is not to make money – though it might lead to some new, as yet unknown, business idea or venture or opportunity.[1] Serendipity or chance in the end always favours those who *do* and persevere at the *doing*.

The second notion (and the central theme in the book) is that entrepreneurship is concerned with being resourceful: the utilisation of resources to create *added value* i.e. not simply an aggregate of what has gone before. For those of a mathematical bent, we could think of entrepreneurship (E) in its simplest form as:

$$E = \Sigma Y + \Sigma P + \Sigma N$$

E being entrepreneurship equals the sum of Y being your resources (attributes, knowledge and skills), with the sum of P being people you know (or more importantly *should* know) and their resources and lastly, with the sum of N being nature's resources (physical, biological, IT, mechanical, environmental). Entrepreneurship is resource based and resource driven.

The third notion is that that we can teach both *about* and *for* the 'lifeworld' of entrepreneurship; that we learn by doing or practising. In many, if not most, of the examples contained in this book individuals started along a path (what motivated them, what they believed in) and learned as they went along. There was no formal business plan as such but an inner belief that this was the right thing to do and a rough mental route map of a path to beat. We are all shaped by our genes and have our behaviours largely shaped for us (through family and peers) but education, experience and opportunity are great levellers. As you learn and then practise your art or craft you become more skilled at doing so. Critically, most people can learn from their mistakes or failings. In time, you become a more polished and successful entrepreneur.

The fourth principle concerns your *art* or *craft*; basically, what are you interested in, what stimulates your learning which in turn develops what you are good at. You find meaning in life by the work that you do. If you want to make your first million then may I suggest (having bought the book) you give it to a friend and buy a book with a title along the lines of '*How I made my first million...*' I am not decrying or denigrating the importance of being business savvy and gaining business experience but merely re-stating the position that fulfilment and meaningful work **and** a life worth living will come from following what you are interested in (what you are good at) to produce added value in society. There is a well-worked cliché of developing or having a passion but this takes time and comes with age (i.e. experience). For the moment it is following your nose and starting from the basis of your intuition of what you think will create added value. Albert Einstein is reported to have written the following: 'A new idea comes suddenly and in a rather intuitive way. But, intuition is nothing but the outcome of earlier intellectual experience'[2]. So the formula of 'success' is education and experience. In short, there is no shortcut to entrepreneurship – it is an apprenticeship of life itself.

The last tenet concerns business ethics and invokes two fundamental principles of biomedical ethics[3] namely non-maleficence and beneficence. The principle of nonmaleficence places an obligation on you in your business dealings not to harm intentionally. It is closely associated with the medical maxim of *Primum non nocere*: 'Above all else (first) do no harm'. This notion of harm extends from people to animals and to the environment. In a fair and just society, the existence of a moral code requires that not only should we not harm people (animals and environments) but also contribute to their general welfare; examples in which we attempt to solve a problem i.e. examples of beneficial action fall under the heading of beneficence. Most entrepreneurs start off with a positive act or thought: "how can I improve the current way of doing things?" or through observation of a 'market failure' or gap, "we don't have this range of products/services at the moment".

Scott Berkin writing in *The Myths of Innovation* stated: 'Today, and for a long time, the majority of what most people believe about ideas—from where they originate to how they are made into things that change the world—is based on sketchy sources. We watch movies featuring the success stories, and we hear legendary tales of geniuses and their flashes of insight, tales passed down from generation to generation, but few go back to see whether any of those stories actually happened. And when we try to work with ideas ourselves, we experience a reality so distant from what we've been taught to expect that it's easy to give up. Even if we fight through the confusion, we're chasing our guesses about what the process is supposed to be like'[4]. My task, through the stories of odd-coupling, is to shed some light on idea creation and take the guess-work out of this thinking on innovation.

Arthur Koestler's works often read as primers for post-graduate studies in philosophy offering little to our subject of enterprise and entrepreneurship; his books are heavy going. Yet there is a kernel in his work *The Act of Creation* that I want to pick up on: the concept of 'bisociation'[5]. Incidentally, the word didn't really take on as you won't find it in the OED and the software programme I am writing in doesn't seem to like it either. Koestler believed that bisociation – the 'sudden interlocking of two previously unrelated skills or matrices of thought' lay at the root of all creation. Furthermore, creative acts cannot be merely conjured up from nothing or nowhere but 'uncovers, selects, re-shuffles, **combines**...already existing facts, ideas, faculties, skills'. *Odd-coupling* in entrepreneurship is precisely this: the conscious (and sometimes accidental) selection, re-shuffling and combination of two seemingly un-related resources to create a new product, service or way of doing things (a cultural artefact). More specifically, my definition of odd-coupling is 'the unusual and innovative application of the characteristics of one resource in combination with another resource to solve a problem or need to create a business'*. It is interesting to note that the term bisociation resonates with the concept of effectuation or effectual logic[6] whereby entrepreneurs start with (limited) means to achieve an, as yet, unknown goal; basically, this stands causal logic on its head, as you start with a clearly defined goal and go get the means to achieve it. Entrepreneurs use this common logic or thinking process at the early stage of business or venture creation. It is also a method which it is argued can be learned and used to 'fuel more effective experiments'[7]. In line with this thinking, the

---

* By business, I simply mean a customer who is interested in your product, service or know-how; its contribution to society can be in and one (or a combination of) health, social, environmental, community, cultural and economic fields

future emerges from our thinking, visioning, experimenting with the (re)combination of resources.

Koestler expanded on bisociation to include 'the creative leap which connects previously connected frames of reference and makes us experience reality on several planes at once.' Is that what entrepreneurs can do when they are doodling or day-dreaming? I think that Koestler will need to be in our *Entrepreneurs Hall of Fame* for another two reasons: his take on serendipity and his ideas on creative anarchy, which I am sure that you will agree these are two pretty good reasons to be included.

It was Louis Pasteur who came up with the phrase that fortune favours the prepared mind (it was actually: 'chance only favours intervention for minds which are prepared for discoveries by patient study and persevering efforts'). Pasteur who was working on substrates of tartrate that become affected by mould, turned an accident into an experiment which in time led him to the recognition that micro-organisms play an essential role in the economy of nature and eventually to his epoch making discoveries in the field of infectious diseases. To pick one more example of serendipity from the end of the nineteenth century, Wilhelm Konrad Röntgen, Professor of Physics at the University of Würzburg noticed by accident that a piece of paper screen covered with barium platinocyanide became fluorescent without any apparent cause. Within a few weeks, Röntgen went on to demonstrate that such rays could pass through dense substances even the human body to provide an outline of the skeletal frame; he named them X-rays. For this discovery, he was awarded the first Nobel prize in 1901. The point I am trying to elaborate here that entrepreneurs don't simply create their 'business' out of nothing, they have knowledge, 'know-how' in an art or a craft in which they are both pursuing and persevering, making mistakes, learning as they go along, taking risks and can 'exploit' in time any accident that comes their way. Fortune or chance will favour them, if and only if, their mind is sensitised to seeing a connection between experiences or events and linking (combining) things together creatively. Koestler saw that contained within the germ of discovery was both a disruptive and construct characteristic; the view was that once an association had been made, it changed the way we would look at the same resource again – in a sense it disrupted the 'rigid pattern of mental processes and disrupts the conventional view'.

When President Barack Obama welcomed the UK Prime Minister David Cameron in 2012, he observed that it was well-nigh impossible to omit a reference to Winston Churchill and to call upon his excerpts of his great speeches to use as an example of the need to have a moral compass in times of great upheaval. In the same vein, a writer on enterprise and entrepreneurship could not fail to acknowledge the influence of an Austrian economist, one Joseph Schumpeter, who apart from a fine name, gave insight into the disruptive elements of economic development[8]. Schumpeter was arguably the first person to draw out a clear concept of entrepreneurship: he differentiated between invention and innovation. He realised that whilst replicative entrepreneurs see an opportunity to apply a new invention, entrepreneurs introduce new means of production, new products and new forms of organisation. As these new forms come into existence, they challenge existing technologies, skills and equipment; some of these may become obsolete. This process was termed 'creative destruction' – a feature if not a necessity for capitalism to work.

An illustration of the role of the Schumpeterian entrepreneur versus that of an effective and efficient manager can be given in terms of the production function. Where a good manager combines the input factors in the production function to achieve the highest technical efficiency, the entrepreneur shifts the production function outward by his innovations. Hence, the entrepreneur moves the economic system out of the static equilibrium by creating new products or production methods thereby rendering others obsolete. This is the process of 'creative destruction' which Schumpeter saw as the driving force behind economic development.

To summarise, our efforts are directed to producing some value in society (social, health economic, environmental). An entrepreneur has to tap into known and yet to be identified resources on three levels namely personal skills, networking and contextual. Through the practice of odd-coupling, we mix up and recombine the characteristics of these resources to produce something innovative which disrupts the present way of living, seeing and doing. Luck or happenchance will undoubtedly play a part but only if our minds are prepared or sensitive to what we see or what we are exposed to. You have to be in the right place, with the right people at the right time. I hope you get there.

Adieu:
'A diagram and a step'

I would like to start my adieu with a fairly lengthy quote from the work of a scientist named Jacob Bronowski. 'Knowledge makes prodigious journeys and what seems to us as a leap in time often turns out be a long progression from place to place, from one city to another...As one example among many, the mathematics of Pythagoras has not come to us directly. It fired the imagination of the Greeks, but the place where it was formed into an orderly system was the Nile city, Alexandria. The man who made the system, and made it famous, was Euclid, who probably took it to Alexandria around 300 BC. Euclid evidently belonged to the Pythagorean tradition. When a listener asked him what was the practical use of some theorem, Euclid is reported to have said contemptuously to his slave, 'He wants profit from learning - give him a penny'. The reproof was probably adapted from a motto of the Pythagorean brotherhood, which translates roughly as 'A diagram and a step – not a diagram and a penny- a 'step' being a step in knowledge or what I have called the Ascent of Man'.

In one sense this book has been about a series of diagrams and steps. I made the very deliberate decision to start each chapter with a drawing, picture or some sort of visual play. The visual became in turn a basis or catalyst for further thought, action and development. The entrepreneur also has a thirst for knowledge both of a *generalist* nature (the context of the idea) but also a deep technical knowledge (the belief that it can work in practice). As with Euclid, we pursue knowledge for its own sake and not for the profit it will bring.

In the promotion of 'real science' as opposed to 'bad science', Ben Goldacre makes an impassioned plea for us all to contribute in some form to the body of valid scientific evidence.[2] He declares: '*You will do this because you know that knowledge is beautiful, and because if only a hundred people share your passion, that is enough*'.

There are a host of books that have influenced the writing of this book – most of which would not be found under an 'Enterprise and Entrepreneurship' section in a book shop (*The Empty Raincoat* by Charles Handy, *Shop class as Soulcraft* by Mathew B Crawford, *The Undercover Economist* by Tim Harford, the rather 'murky' side of entrepreneurship in *The White Tiger* by Aravind Adiga and so on) but there is one book that stands out as first among equals and that it the work of Janine Benyus. In *Biomimicry*, she expounds on the innumerate examples of innovation we can derive from nature – nature as **model**. She also examines nature both as a **measure** (to judge the "rightness" of our innovations) and as a **mentor** (to teach us to not only to extract but to learn from the natural world). It is a simple but compelling principle for us all to adopt and adapt in entrepreneurial learning and entrepreneurship.

My emphasis in the book has been 'upstream', that is on idea generation through a method of odd-coupling: the (re) combining of resources to create something, maintain something that is working well or fix something that isn't. However, all the ideas presented in this book have been "taken to market" in one form of another: each idea has resulted in a product or service which has (at least one!) buyer or user. The point being is that idea generation has a twin track objective. In the first case, the process of generating ideas can help in the process of generating *better* ideas; secondly, an idea has a further utility in the *value* it creates in society. Your entrepreneurial ideas will have both such components. In Tom Harford's words, you will be contributing to an *efficient* market whereby someone gains something, you "sell" it and no one is harmed in the transaction. [3]

I realise that to get your idea to market takes another set of attributes, behaviours and skills. It will require determination and perseverance ('blood, sweat and tears'), the simple notion of your devoted time in abundance, the risk to family and social groupings, of doing without – all for something in the *future* which might not work out! But once you start on this journey of using and applying your knowledge, interest and *identifying* the vital resources the business will need, the task is to get hold of these resources, (re) use and (re) combine them and try for yourself. Life should not be one of regret – looking back and thinking, "I had this really good idea….but". As the saying goes, we only get one life.

Co-development

In the spirit of co-development of ideas, I have set up an odd-coupling website in which you can provide examples of odd-coupling in entrepreneurship. At the time of going to press, the supermarket giant Waitrose had set up an interactive sight for its patrons to comment (tweet) on their new service. The responses were varied, some quite amusing, others though quite harmless were certainly not acceptable and so the supermarket was quick to pull the plug on the interactive sight. For this reason, I have placed a proviso that all contributions will be 'vetted' to make sure that they are not in any way offensive. Moreover, I will acknowledge all accepted contributions on the site. You can find the site at **www.odd-coupling.co.uk** If we get anywhere near Goldacre's hundred responses and contributions (and share my interest) then that would be a good contribution to the 'project' of amassing knowledge and understanding on the concept of odd-coupling.

I want to leave on a positive note: ideas are infinite and (most of the time) can lead to a sustainable good. I want to recall the thoughts of Richard Jacobs author of *Searching for Beauty* who believes in the beauty and importance of craft. He opined the separation of craft from art and design; in short, there is a danger in the separation of 'having ideas' from 'making objects'. This separation, he believed solidified a general principle that there exists some sort of mental attribute known as creativity that precedes or can be divorced from knowledge of how things work and how to make things.[4]

In this vein, if I am allowed one 'left field' idea, it is this: allow all primary school children the opportunity to make **and** fly a kite – not buy a pre-made entity but make from scratch. They can record, how it was made, how it flew, fell, crashed, repaired and flew again. It will put them literally in touch with nature and basic engineering. But and here is the big but: they have learned to master in some small way the critically important link between brain and hand and have learned something about an infinite resource (the wind). They have learned how to respect, use and perhaps harness one of the earth's resources. They should all receive a certificate (alongside proficiency in swimming) to state that they mastered this critical life skill. Children will then have made their own 'diagram and a step'.

Let all our young minds fly

References

I have kept the number of references down to a reasonable minimum level. I wanted to show that I wasn't simply 'haverin', or trying to elucidate a general principle of creativity around mere anecdote but, provide a reasonable 'body' of evidence to show that it is a credible concept and worth pursuing.

Introduction

1   **Terkel S,** *Work: People talk about what they do all day and how they feel about what they do* The New Press. New York 1970
2   **Paley SJ,** *The Art of Invention – the creative process of discovery and design* Prometheus Books New York 2012
3   **Benyus JM,** *Biomimicry- Innovation inspired* by nature Harper New York 1997
4   **Gladwell M** *Outliers, The story of success* Penguin New York 2007

Chapter 1

1   Landmines, the human cost ADF Health Vol 1 1 September 2000
2   International Committee of the Red Cross 1996, UN mining database
3   International Physicians for the Prevention of Nuclear War. IPPNW Global Healthwatch Second Report Landmines: a global health crisis. 1997.
4   **Quignon P,** et al *The dog and rat olfactory receptor repertoire* Genome Biology 2005 6:R83
5   **Benyus JM,** *Biomimicry Innovation* inspired by nature Harper New York 1997
6   TED Ideas worth spreading Presented June 2010 http://www.ted.com/talks/lang/en/bart_weetjens

Chapter 2

1 For the basics of baseball see http://www. howbaseballworks.com/TheBasics.htm

2 **Lewis M,** *Moneyball* Norton New York 2004

3 For further information see The Office of the Comptroller of the Currency at http://occ.gov/topics/capital-markets/financial-markets/trading/derivatives/index-derivatives.html

4 Top 10 Influencers in The Business of Sports see http://www.forbes.com/sites/sap/2012/05/23/top-10-influencers-in-the-business-of-sports/

Chapter 3

1 The Caspian tigers used to be found from Western China all the way to Turkey and was determined extinct in the 60s or 70s. But recently genetic analysis shows that Caspian tigers are very similar to Siberian Tigers

2 The IUCN red list still considers it to be critically endangered

3 This predicament refers not only India and Russia but throughout countries where the tiger existed. The wild tiger population has drastically declined and some reserves are practically devoid of tigers over in the past decade.

4 Dr. Ian Player saved the white rhino in South Africa by doing similar, but considered probably at the extreme end of animal conservation. He sold some of the few remaining white rhino from games reserves in Kwa-Zulu Natal to open zoos in UK and US, apart from moving some others to other reserves in SA to save them from potential hardship in 1960s. The white rhino now numbers 20,000 in South Africa, all descended from the rhinos he saved. By comparison, Li has provided the South China tigers a different, more positive future.

5   Tiger finance, a banker's effort to fund survival, Reuters, Feb 16 2011

6   Gus Mills, Research Fellow: SAN Parks / Head Carnivore Conservation Group: EWT (Issued press release on behalf of five organization on 14th November 2003

7   BBC Radio Four Return of the South China Tiger Tuesday 28th February 2012 (http://www.bbc.co.uk/programmes/b01cjwtl)

Chapter 4

1   **Schieber A, Saldana M,** Potato Peels: A source of nutrition and pharmacologically interesting compounds - A Review Food 3 (Special Issue 2) Global Science Books 2009.

2   **Singh N, Kamath V, Rajini PS**, Protective effect of potato peel powder in ameliorating oxidative stress in streptozotocin diabetic rats Plant Foods for Human Nutrition 60,49-54

3   **Singh N, Kamath V**, Rajini PS Attenuation of hyperglycemia and associated parameters in STZ-induced rats by supplementation of potato peel power Clinica Chimica Acta 353,166-175

4. **McGraw k, Horak P, Constantini D, Cohen A,** (eds) *Antioxidants and oxidative stress in animals* British Ecological Society London September 2012

5   **Keswani MH, Vartak AM, Patil A, Davies JW**, Histological and bacteriological studies of burn wounds treated with boiled potato peel dressings. Burns. 1990 Apr;16(2):137-43.

6   **Subrahmanyam M**, Honey dressing versus boiled potato peel in the treatment of burns: a prospective randomized study Burns 1996 Sep;22(6):491-3.

7   **Vlachojannis, J. E., Cameron, M. and Chrubasik, S**,
    (2010), Medicinal use of potato-derived products: a
    systematic review. Phytotherapy Research, 24: 159–162.
    doi: 10.1002/ptr.28298

8   **De Buck E**, *Potato peel dressings for wound burns* 12
    January 2010 Best Evidence Topics (http://www.bestbets.
    org/bets/bet.php?id=1876)

9   See *Burnsurgery.com* website for a list of modules on burn
    surgery, treatment and care

Chapter 5

1   For those of a disbelieving nature see http://www.
    shedblog.co.uk/2012/07/03/shed-week-guest-post-shed-
    inventors/

2   **Levenstein S**, *Wasabi Smoke Alarm Wins* 2011 Ig Nobel
    Prize Inventor Spot 2011

3   Seems Inc., Tokyo http://www.seems-inc.com

4   *Personal correspondence with Professor Makoto Imai* 18
    March 2012; 12 September 2012

5   **Allman BL, Keniston LP, Meredith MA**, Adult deafness
    induces somatosensory conversion of ferret auditory
    cortex. Proc Natl Acad Sci U S A. 2009 Apr 7;106
    (14):5925-30. Epub 2009 Mar 23

6   Got a burning throat. Quick! The house may be on fire.
    News The Times 12 March 2012

Chapter 6

1   The World Health Organisation. Facts on Asthma http://
    www.who.int/mediacentre/factsheets/fs307/en/index.html
    accessed 26 Match 2012

2   *Guidance for Industry Metered Dose Inhaler (MDI) and
    Dry Powder Inhaler (DPI) Drug Products Chemistry,
    Manufacturing, and Controls Documentation* Draft

Guidance U.S. Department of Health and Human Services Food and Drug Administration Center for Drug Evaluation and Research (CDER) October 1998

3   **David Harris**, *Choosing the right device: the case for DPIs* Team consulting Cambridge UK December 2011

4   **Hannaway, Paul**, *What To Do When The Doctor Says Its Asthma: Everything You Need to Know About Medicines, Allergies, Food and Exercise to Breathe More Easily Every Day* Gloucester, MA: F

f Rex McCandless Ulster Folk and Transport Museum 1989

2   See http://thevintagent.blogspot.co.uk/2008/12/rex-mccandless-and-featherbed-frame.html

3   **Crawford D**, *Stanley Woods – The World's First Motorcycle Superstar* Crawford Publishing 2011

Chapter 9

1   *Jimi Heselden: Miner who used his redundancy money to become a businessman and philanthropist* The Independent Saturday 2 October 2010

2   *Link Gabions and Mattresses Design Booklet Global* Synthetics Queensland Australia 2010

3   General Motors shoes vision of urban mobility 10 July 2011

    see http://www.bbc.co.uk/news/business-14060276

4   What is the car of tomorrow? See http://www.earthtechling.com/2012/04/gm-en-v-2-0-people-mover-continues-tomorrowland-vision/

5   Leeds Community Foundation 51A St Paul's Street, Leeds, West Yorkshire, LS1 2TE

Chapter 10

1   **Kay J**, *Obliquity – why our goals are best achieved indirectly* Profile Books London 2010

2 **Hudson K**, *The Idea Generator -60 Tools for Business Growth* Atlantic Books London 2008

3 UNESCO Archives and Records Management 1985

Chapter 11

1 **Stewart D**, *The Light in The Tunnel* www. dougstewartonline

2 Road Safety Award *Highways and Transportation* No5 Vol 31 1984

3 **Stewart D**, *A clearer vision for pedestrian guardrails* Pages 131–136 Proceedings of Institute of Civil Engineers. Civil Engineering 160 No CE3 August 2007

4 Department for Transport, Communities and Local Government and Welsh Assembly Government. *Manual for Streets*. Thomas Telford, London, 2007

5 **Jha A**, *Does removing road markings reduce accidents?* The Guardian, Thursday 27 May 2004

6 **GEHL J**, *Towards a Fine City for People—Public Spaces and Public Life—*London 2004. Gehl Architects ApS, Copenhagen, Denmark, 2004

7 **Webster B**, *Naked streets are safer, say the Tories* The Times 22 January 2007

8 Imperial College London The naked street: Imperial engineers help revitalise famous road in London's cultural hub www.imperial.ac.uk

Chapter 12

1 Old Street, London see for instance *Tech City: the magic roundabout* The Guardian Sunday 27 November 2011

2 Patient knows best http://www.patientsknowbest.com/index.html

3 The Electronic Patient Record. House of Commons Health Committee. Sixth Report of Session 2006–07. Volume I. 13

September 2007. London: The Stationery Office Limited
4   Personal correspondence Dr Julian Brown 13 September 2012

Chapter 13

1   Oxford English Dictionary 2nd Edition Oxford University Press Northampton 2010
2   **Naar N, Jenkins S**, *The Birth of Graffiti* Prestel London 2007
3   **Burgess A**, *A Clockwork Orange* Penguin London 1962
4   **Heyman L**, *The Thomas Crown Affair* Hodder Paperbacks London 1968
     Wright S, *Banksy's Bristol: Home Sweet Home* Tangent Books London 2008
5   **Wright S**, *Home Sweet Home Banky's Bristol* Tangent Books Bristol UK 2007
     Art of the state http://www.artofthestate.co.uk
6   See also **Bull M**, *Banksy Locations and Tours: Revised and Updated for 2008: A Collection of Graffiti Locations and Photographs in London* Shellshock Publishing 2008

Chapter 14

1   **Levi P**, *The Periodic Table* Abacus London 1975
2   **Savage N**, *Materials science: Super carbon Nature* 483 S30–S31 (15 March 2012) doi:10.1038/483S30 Published online 14 March 2012
3   See the nanotube website http://www.pa.msu.edu/cmp/csc/nanotube.html
4   Condensed Matter Physics Group University of Manchester (http://www.condmat.physics.manchester.ac.uk/)
5   **Park H**, et al 2010 *Doped graphene electrodes for organic solar cells* Nanotechnology 21 Number 50 5doi:10.1088/0957-4484/21/50/505204

6   **Li J, Chung TF, Chen YP, Cheng G**, *Nanoscale Strainability of Graphene by Laser Shock Induced 3D Shaping* Nano Letters 12, 4577 (2012)

7. National Endowment for Science, Technology and The Arts http://www.nesta.org.uk/news_and_features/assets/features/andre_geim_and_kostya_novoselov

Chapter 15

1   **H W Dickinson**, *Matthew Boulton* Cambridge University Press Cambridge 1936

2   Alas, there is no record of this partnership in legal terms; perhaps it was simply done on trust

3   39.Geo.III,1799, cap 96

Epilogue

1   This is known as the 'lemonade principle' in the concept of effectuation – but I deal with this later on in the chapter

2   **Isaacson W**, *Einstein: His Life and Universe* Simon & Schuster New York 2007

3   **Beauchamp & Childress**, *Principles of Biomedical Ethics* 4th Edit Oxford University Press New York 1994

4   **Berkin S**, *The Myths of Innovation* O'Reilly Media Inc. New York 2010

5   **Koestler A**, *The Act of Creation* Pan Books Ltd London 1964

6   **Sarasvathy S**, *Effectuation: elements of entrepreneurial expertise* Edward Elgar Publishing UK 2008

7   See for instance the Society for Effectual Action at http://www.effectuation.org/

8   **Schumpeter J**, *Theory of Economic Development* Leipzig: Duncker and Humblot. Translated by R. Opie 1911. Cambridge: Harvard University Press

1   **Bronowski J**, *The Ascent of Man* Back Bay Books Boston 1973

2   **Goldacre B**, *Bad Science* Fourth Estate London 2008

3   **Harford T**, *The Undercover Economist* Abacus London 2007

4   **Jacobs R**, *In Search of Beauty* Kestrel Books Wales UK 2007

CPSIA information can be obtained at www.ICGtesting.com
Printed in the USA
LVOW011143180413

3454LVUK00015B/32/P